W9-CMP-701

Eating Disorders

Look for these and other books in the Lucent Overview Series:

Abortion
Adoption
Advertising
AIDS
Alcoholism
The Beginning of Writing
Cancer
Censorship
Child Abuse
Cities
Civil Liberties
Cloning
Cults
Dealing with Death
The Death Penalty
Democracy
Depression
Diabetes
Drug Abuse
Drugs and Sports
Drug Trafficking
Eating Disorders
Elections
Epidemics
Espionage
Ethnic Violence
Euthanasia
Gangs

Gay Rights
Hate Groups
Hazardous Waste
Health Care
Homeless Children
Homelessness
The Internet
Juvenile Crime
Medical Ethics
Mental Illness
Militias
Money
Obesity
The Olympic Games
Paranormal Phenomena
Police Brutality
Poverty
Schools
School Violence
Sexual Harassmen
Space Exploration
Sports in America
Suicide
The U.S. Congress
The U.S. Presidency
Violence Against Women
Women's Rights
World Hunger

Eating Disorders

by Jennifer L. Strada

Lucent
Books

Thanks to Al, Berylann,
Melissa, and Amy

Library of Congress Cataloging-in-Publication Data

Strada, Jennifer L., 1970–
    Eating disorders / by Jennifer L. Strada.
      p.   cm. — (Lucent overview series)
Includes bibliographical references and index.
    ISBN 1-56006-659-8
    1. Eating disorders—Juvenile literature.   [1. Eating disorders.]
    I. Title.   II. Series.
      RC552.E18 S774   2001
      616.85'26—dc21   00-010392

No part of this book may be reproduced or used in any form or by any means, electrical,
mechanical, or otherwise, including, but not limited to, photocopy, recording, or any information storage and retrieval system, without prior written permission from the publisher.

Copyright © 2001 by Lucent Books, Inc.
P.O. Box 289011, San Diego, CA 92198-9011
Printed in the U.S.A.

Contents

Introduction

FOOD NOURISHES AND sustains the human body. It energizes the body with nutrients that keep it strong and healthy. Food is also a source of pleasure, whether one is dining out in a favorite restaurant or sitting down for a home-cooked meal.

Yet for many, food is a source of conflict and a daily obsession. For these people, the act of eating—or not eating—is not an issue of body nourishment or hunger. Instead, it is a way to express or cope with feelings. It is also a fixation that can take total control over a person's behavior. When someone's relationship with food affects his or her self-esteem, sense of identity, or ability to be happy, that person has what is known as an eating disorder.

Eating disorders are a very serious health problem in the United States. As many as 10 million people or more suffer from them, and that number seems to be on the rise. At the same time, doctors report that the average age of eating disorder patients has been dropping, with both children and adults proving vulnerable.

Secretive behavior

During the development of her book *Ophelia Speaks*, author Sara Shandler sent an open invitation to adolescent girls across the country, asking them to submit their own opinions on various issues facing girls today. Over eight hundred girls, from diverse backgrounds, contributed. Among the concerns addressed, the most written-about subject was eating disorders.

Eating disorders are characterized by self-destructive behavior, but one danger in these illnesses is that unhealthy eating habits are usually carried out secretively. This means that detecting an eating disorder in a family member or friend is not always easy, and substantial harm can occur before others become aware of the problem.

While eating disorders are psychological in nature, they can be extremely harmful to a person's physical health— possibly even fatal. In fact, of all mental or emotional

In an effort to hide their illness, persons with eating disorders carry out self-destructive activities in a secluded place.

illnesses, eating disorders have the highest fatality rate. It is estimated that about one in five patients with eating disorders dies prematurely; among those who die from eating disorders, heart problems are the leading cause of death.

There are several treatment options for those struggling with eating disorders, the most common being some form of therapy. But with eating disorders afflicting so many Americans, the need for prevention seems to be more urgent than ever.

Influence of the media

In considering the causes of eating disorders and the ways to prevent them, one great concern among many eating disorder experts is that American culture is partly to blame for the spread of these illnesses. Anyone who watches television or reads magazines can see or hear the media's messages about how bodies should look. These messages suggest—sometimes subtly and sometimes more directly—that a particular body type is desirable, and this puts pressure on both males and females to look a certain way. Many doctors see these messages as laying the groundwork for developing an eating disorder.

Given the influence of mass media, it is no coincidence that the diet industry is thriving in the United States, with billions of dollars spent each year on diet products and programs. Whether for health-related or cosmetic reasons, dieting has become a common practice for many Americans. Yet while some diets may be balanced and healthy, others may be a form of nutritional deprivation. Moreover, for some people, the difference between a diet and an eating disorder becomes blurred. They may not realize that their eating or exercise habits are unhealthy, or they may simply be kidding themselves when it comes to their eating habits.

Educating oneself about eating disorders can clarify how eating disorders develop, who is particularly vulnerable, the behavioral warning signs of each kind of disorder, and how those who suffer can be helped.

1

An Obsession
with Food

FOR MANY PEOPLE in today's society, dieting has
become not just a special way of eating but a way of life.
Once practiced by relatively few Americans for specific
medical conditions, dieting is now a common part of
American culture. In fact, surveys indicate that at any one
time, about 45 percent of women and 25 percent of men
are dieting. In some cases, what starts as a healthy attempt
at weight loss turns into an eating disorder.

The line between a normal concern about food and appearance and an abnormal obsession is not easily defined.
At what point does a diet turn into an eating disorder? According to the authors of *Surviving an Eating Disorder*,
"An eating disorder exists when one's attitude toward food
and weight has gone awry—when one's feelings about
work, school, relationships, day-to-day activities, and one's
experience of emotional well-being are determined by what
has or has not been eaten or by a number on the scale." Although many people turn to food as a source of comfort or
as a reward—even while simultaneously wishing that they
could lose a few pounds—it is "when these wishes or re-
wards turn into the basis of all decisions . . . then there are
indications of a problem deserving attention."[1]

Eating disorders pose a major health problem in the
United States. It is estimated that 5 to 10 million girls and
women and 1 million boys and men have eating disorders.
The three main types of eating disorders are anorexia

nervosa, bulimia nervosa, and binge eating disorder (also known as compulsive overeating). While each disorder is associated with unique behaviors and health consequences, the common characteristic of these disorders is an obsessive attitude toward food.

When no amount of weight loss is enough

Anorexia nervosa develops when a person's desire to lose weight, even if it began with a healthy regimen of diet and exercise, turns into an obsessive and unhealthy pattern of self-starvation. Like many who set out to lose weight by dieting, anorexics set a goal of becoming thin and staying thin. But then the goal becomes a fixation. Despite any weight loss that results from a particular regimen, anorexics remain dissatisfied with their weight or body shape—to the point that no amount of weight loss is enough. Eventually, unless someone intervenes, the weight loss becomes harmful to their health.

The three most common eating disorders are:	
anorexia	preoccupation with dieting and thinness leading to excessive weight loss
bulimia	frequent episodes of binge eating followed by purging
binge eating	compulsive overeating without purging

Even if anorexics maintain abnormally low body weights, they still feel an irrational fear of gaining weight. They also have an unrealistic image of their bodies. Anorexics always believe that they are too fat—and they focus constantly on how they can lose more weight or achieve what they see as a more appealing body shape. Eventually their diets become so strict that they begin to starve their bodies of the nutrients needed to stay healthy.

When anorexics first start dieting, they might follow a moderate diet that does not seem out of the ordinary. With a goal of losing just a few pounds, they begin a low-calorie or low-fat diet. Anorexics, after they lose a small amount of weight from dieting, want to lose even more weight, and they become obsessed with how diet—and often exercise as well—can help them reach an ever-changing goal.

Whatever the underlying causes of their problems, many anorexics believe that being thin will bring them happiness. Explains one recovering anorexic, "Whenever I wished for anything, I wished to be skinny. I just knew that if I was skinny, all my problems would be solved. I would be beautiful. I wouldn't have to be afraid—I could be just what I wanted."[2] Of course, most problems are not solved by losing weight. If anorexics lose the weight they initially set out to lose, they are still not happy. Believing that achieving a greater weight loss will make them happier, their daily life starts to revolve around losing still more weight. As anorexics become fixated on losing weight and the feeling that straying from their diet is "wrong," a vicious cycle develops—one that can be difficult to escape from.

Weight loss as a source of pride

Above all, anorexics fear weight gain. For an anorexic, any weight gain signifies a loss of control, which in turn creates a sense of failure. One doctor explains that anorexics "feel confident if they are losing weight and worthless and guilty if they are not. . . . No one can make them gain weight. Their thinness has become a source of pride, a badge of honor."[3]

People with anorexia never feel thin enough, even when friends or family members express concern about their unhealthy appearance.

One anorexic describes the difficulty of breaking out of this mindset:

> A pound today means another tomorrow, if I don't cut back. If I've gained a pound, it means I'm gaining, so I have to stop eating and then I start losing. I don't want to lose, but I can't stand it when I look at the scale and I've gained. Once I reach a certain weight, like 95 pounds or so, I can never go above that weight. I don't know why."[4]

A constant battle with food

Since the main goal of anorexics is to lose weight, they view food as something to avoid whenever possible.

Their relationship with food becomes a constant battle. They stop thinking of food as a source of nutrition and energy, and as a consequence, they avoid eating even when hungry. When they do have a meal or snack, they do not enjoy eating and feel guilty afterward for having gone off their diets.

Despite their fear of eating too much, almost half of all anorexics are not able to maintain the strict diets they have set for themselves and experience episodes of binge eating. Bingeing involves eating unusually large amounts of food quickly within a short period of time. Under such circumstances, an anorexic feels a complete loss of control. One eating disorder patient says that bingeing is "like being in a stupor, like being drunk. Nothing else matters. Heaven help the person who tries to stop me. It's like I'm a different person."[5]

Weight gain seen as lacking self-discipline

Unfortunately, an eating binge can lead to still more anorexic behavior. After bingeing, anorexics may feel even more unhappy with their weight and with what they see as their lack of self-discipline. Thus, they continue with their anorexic behavior—sometimes at a greater intensity—to make up for the binge and to lose the weight again. Some anorexics who binge may also purge what they have eaten, which means using an unnatural method —such as self-induced vomiting—to remove food and calories from the body.

Generally, anorexics are secretive about their behaviors. In part, this is because eating makes them feel guilty and ashamed. Moreover, keeping their eating habits under wraps allows anorexics to maintain a sense of control over one aspect of their lives. One recovering anorexic recalls, "I'm thinking to myself, 'Ha, ha. You don't know what I'm really like. I have an ugly, horrible secret, and it's more ugly and horrible than all that fat I lost.' But it's comfortable. And I keep it a secret. Because it's all that I've got."[6]

Ironically, although they view food as an enemy that might prevent them from losing weight, many anorexics show signs of being obsessed with food. Some may create special rules or rituals for eating, such as when and where they can eat, choosing which foods they are allowed to eat, or determining how their food is prepared or presented. As one doctor explains, "An anorexic may start out by allowing herself only a certain number of calories each day. Then she may make a rule that the only foods she can eat are yogurt and fresh fruits. She may decide that each piece of fruit must be carefully divided into six pieces, or some other 'magic' number, and arranged in a certain way on her plate."[7]

Vicarious pleasure from food

Some anorexics take a vicarious pleasure from food. Anorexics might even enjoy cooking a big dinner for their friends but then barely eat the meal themselves. If they only nibble at the food, they may push it around on the plate to make it look as if they have been eating. Some anorexics talk a lot about food, leading people around them to believe that food is a normal part of their lifestyle while the reality is that they avoid eating.

But for anorexics, more is at stake than just their physical self-perception or their sense of control. Anorexics convince themselves that not eating is an achievement, a sign of success rather than an act of deprivation. One recovering anorexic recalls her relationship with food: "I was hungry, but I didn't think I was depriving myself. I was pretty proud of the tight rein I had on my eating."[8] Such "success," of course, reinforces the anorexic behavior, and the cycle continues.

Some anorexics may also use exercise in their battle against weight gain. They might have a strict exercise schedule that they follow in a very disciplined way. One doctor recalls her anorexic patient who ran at least ten miles each day while her diet consisted only of mushrooms and lettuce. When the patient was advised to stop running because her health was suffering from the combination of excessive exercise and undereating, she replied, "I don't have a choice. There is a voice in my head that says I must

An anorexic often develops a strict exercise routine to lose weight; this schedule can prove fatal when combined with a poor diet.

run faster and farther, even though I know it's not getting me anywhere I want to go." While her commitment to exercise was strong, she did not recognize the importance of eating a healthy diet. She said, "I really don't feel like I need food. I know it's crazy, but running is my food."[9]

If anorexics do not lose weight as desired, or if they eat more food than usual at a meal or during a particular day, then exercise seems like a way to prevent weight gain. This kind of exercise is not healthy, however, because the anorexic's body is already starved of important nutrients. Because anorexia weakens a person's bones and muscles, excessive exercise is stressful to the body and can lead to serious health consequences.

Thinking they can eat whatever they want

When people think of someone suffering from an eating disorder, they often think of an anorexic who is visibly malnourished and underweight. However, bulimia nervosa is actually a more widespread eating disorder. People suffering from bulimia share the anorexic's obsession with body weight and shape.

Like anorexics, bulimics focus excessively on food. They are extremely concerned with how weight affects their physical appearance, and they are intensely afraid of becoming fat. Yet while anorexics starve themselves to lose as much weight as they can, bulimics suffer from an ongoing cycle of bingeing—uncontrollably eating large amounts of food in a brief period of time—and purging—using self-induced vomiting or other ways to rid the body of food eaten during a binge.

Initially bulimics may feel that the cycle of bingeing and purging offers a way to control their weight. Yet the reality is that they are not in control, as they become unable to moderate either their eating or their response to eating. As one doctor explains, at first bulimics think "they can eat whatever they want and get rid of it. Then, after a couple of years, it hits: 'I thought I could stop any time. But I can't.'"[10]

Experts believe that bulimia is a compulsive disorder. When a person involuntarily repeats an action, whether it is consciously desired or not, it is known as a compulsion. Compulsions can entirely dictate a person's behavior. In bulimics, this is apparent in the uncontrollable nature of their bingeing and purging.

Like any eating disorder, bulimia arises for many different reasons. Yet bulimics usually begin the binge-purge cycle during stressful or emotionally difficult times. Experiences like going to a new school, starting a new job, relationship problems, or changes at home can lead to the first episode of bingeing. When their customary situation becomes troubled, bulimics seek comfort in food and then anxiously work to eliminate it, setting off a cycle of bingeing and purging.

Although they share an obsession with food, bulimics and anorexics differ in significant ways. While anorexics are underweight from excessive dieting, bulimics tend to stay within a ten to fifteen pound range of what is considered a normal weight for their age and height. Because they alternate between bingeing and purging, their weight may vary; however, they do not experience the extreme weight loss that anorexics do.

Like anorexics, some bulimics may follow rigid diets when they are not bingeing and purging, but others eat normally without special restrictions. In public they may appear to eat normal meals and follow a healthy diet, yet their secret bingeing and purging is a hidden sign of their obsession with food and their intense fear of becoming overweight.

Eating far beyond feeling full

Because bulimics use food to cope with emotional problems and stress, any strong emotion or stressful experience can trigger a binge. A binge may consist of eating several thousand calories in one sitting, and bulimics tend to eat far beyond the point of feeling full.

Bulimics may binge on any kind of food, though binge foods are often starchy or sweet. They also may be foods that are not a part of the bulimic's usual diet. For example, if they do not eat sweets ordinarily, they may crave them during a binge and eat an excessive amount. Whatever food the bulimics focus on during the binge, they always eat more than would be considered healthy or normal. One study found that bulimic patients "frequently binge-eat foods that they avoid at other times because they fear their high-caloric nature. Other patients, however, binge-eat on what they believe to be more healthy foods (like fresh fruits and vegetables), or they simply turn a regular meal into a binge by enlarging the quantity of food to be eaten." [11] If a bulimic feels the urge to binge, the food choice often involves simply eating the foods that are most accessible at the time—whatever is within reach in the refrigerator or pantry.

Feeling completely out of control

Bulimics describe the experience of bingeing as feeling completely out of control. When bulimics feel emotional stress and experience the urge to binge, they are usually

Bulimics can become trapped by the relentless cycle of bingeing and purging.

unable to resist the temptation. Because they find comfort in the binge food as they eat, rational concerns about the abnormally large amount of food being unhealthy for them do not prevent or shorten the binge. They eat until they feel better emotionally, no matter how long that takes or how much food is eaten.

One doctor says that her bulimic patient "binged twice a day, sometimes three times. She described her binge episodes as being a kind of craziness when she fell into a trance and inhaled whatever was around. Her preferred foods were breads, cereals, and graham crackers, but she ate anything." The patient agreed: "Once I lose control, I'll eat whatever I can find." [12]

Purging

Although bulimics may feel comforted while eating the binge food, immediately afterward they feel guilty and depressed about having overeaten. In a desperate attempt to reverse the binge, bulimics decide to purge the food from their bodies. As one bulimic describes it, "I would start thinking about how much I had eaten, and I would panic. I had to get rid of all that food, so I would make myself throw up." [13]

The two most common methods of purging are self-induced vomiting and the use of laxatives. Bulimics force themselves to vomit by putting their fingers (or another object) in the back of their throat. They might also use ipecac syrup, a drug that is ordinarily used to induce vomiting in children after accidental poisoning. Laxatives, in turn, give bulimics a feeling of having an empty stomach, although they mostly get rid of water weight rather than calories. For bulimics, however, they are just content to feel like their stomachs are no longer full from bingeing.

Bulimics may also attempt to get rid of the excess calories they have consumed by purging the body with diuretics (drugs that increase urination), taking diet pills, fasting, or engaging in crash exercise programs. Whatever the method of purging, the goal is the same: bulimics desperately seek to correct the binge, which they perceive as a terrible mistake.

Persons with bulimia find temporary comfort from bingeing, which quickly becomes a habitual means of dealing with stress or crisis.

But even though purging makes bulimics feel better temporarily, it is just a matter of time before another stressful experience or emotional crisis triggers the next binge.

How often the cycle of bingeing and purging is repeated varies considerably. Some bulimics binge and purge once or twice a week; others go through the cycle several times in one day. Regardless of the frequency, the use of food as a means of responding to emotional or mental stress indicates a relationship with food that has become unhealthy.

Binge eating disorder

Sometimes a person's eating habits include frequent bingeing without the corresponding act of purging. This behavior is called binge eating disorder, also known as compulsive overeating. Like anorexics and bulimics, binge eaters are obsessed with food. Throughout each day, a binge eater's thoughts are focused on their meals and snacks, concerned with what and when they will eat next. They eat in binges—consuming food in abnormally large portions, beyond the point when the stomach feels full and comfortable.

The disorder begins much like a bulimic's first experience with bingeing. A person facing some kind of emotional upset or stress may turn to food for comfort. Bingeing helps the person to forget about whatever emotions or problems are causing the stress, setting up a sort of dependency on food that goes far beyond mere nutrition.

Not unexpectedly, some people with binge eating disorder are also on diets. Extremely aware of their body weight and shape, binge eaters may try to control their food intake in order to keep their weight down. In some cases, however, being on a strict diet actually results in more frequent bingeing. Binge eaters who feel deprived by diets that set rules for which foods and how often they may eat sometimes feel an urge to binge and seek out foods that they are ordinarily restricted from eating.

Eating as an escape

Although binge eaters and bulimics share the common behavior of bingeing, bulimics have a preoccupation with weight loss whereas binge eaters are often more focused on the comfort afforded by the act of eating. One woman remembers that her binge eating disorder developed at a time when she was burdened by problems with her family: "Food seemed to be the only way I could dull the pain. I got into the habit of looking in the mirror, being depressed at what I saw and eating some more so that I could cope. . . . My behavior became destructive to me. I now knew I was using food as an escape from emotional pain and stress."[14]

The dangerous behavior of a binge eater may not be as recognizable as the behavior of an anorexic and a bulimic. As the authors of *Surviving an Eating Disorder* explain, "Without the obviously strange and damaging behavior of vomiting, the binge eater and those around her are less likely to identify her problem as serious. It often seems to her and others that the problem is one of too big an appetite or a stubborn lack of self-control." [15]

Borderline behavior

Not all eating disorders fall exactly under the categories of anorexia nervosa, bulimia nervosa, or binge eating disorder. Some struggling with eating disorders exhibit behavior of more than one type of disorder. Perhaps a person develops one disorder and then eventually begins eating habits associated with another. Because those suffering from eating disorders are confused about their relationship with food and about their body image, their eating patterns are not necessarily consistent over time.

For example, a bulimic obsessed with weight loss may become frustrated with not losing much weight from the cycle of bingeing and purging. As a result, the bulimic might desperately cut back on food consumption, and, in time, his or her behavior could evolve into the eating habits of an anorexic. Likewise, a habitual binge eater might become anxious about the weight gained from bingeing and add purging to the eating cycle in an attempt to compensate for the frequent binges. Thus, the binge eater can seek comfort in binge food while keeping his or her weight somewhat stable by purging—and binge eating disorder turns into bulimia.

One woman recalls her transition from anorexia to bulimia:

> I was anorexic for a year and a half. The initial compliments had turned into comments like, "You look sick," and "You need to eat.". . . A friend who was bulimic told me how she made herself vomit. I thought that if I could still eat but keep the weight off, that would be better than not eating because then I'd have more energy. So I started to make myself vomit. Gradually I ate more and more, and within two months I was throwing up 10 times a day. [16]

Whether a person is an anorexic, a bulimic, or a binge eater, at the heart of the illness is an unhealthy relationship

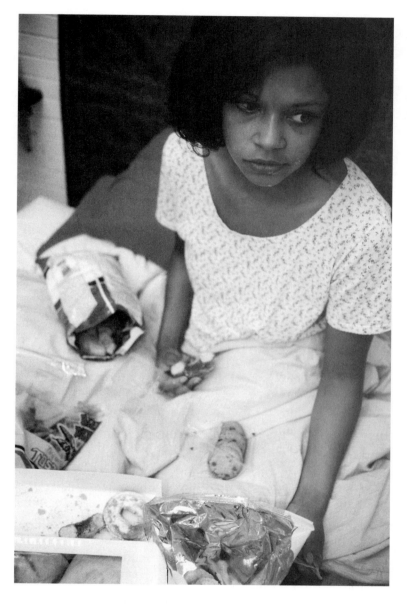

with food and a struggle to accept his or her body. To understand how a simple diet can turn into an eating disorder, one must consider all of the influences around a person—from family and friends to work or school environments to what he or she watches on television—and how these influences can affect that person's ideas about food, body image, and self-esteem.

2

The Causes and Risk Factors of Eating Disorders

IT CAN BE difficult to identify the single origin of an eating disorder. Eating disorders can develop from a number of different causes, ranging from psychological to biological to even cultural factors, yet most are rooted in a person's self-image and emotional stability. An eating disorder can be a way of coping with low self-esteem, emotional problems, or other personal issues. Affecting men, women, boys, and girls alike, the widespread problem of eating disorders also raises questions about the role of society in shaping body image.

For some people, biological factors may make them prone to eating disorders. Research has found that certain chemical levels in the brain, those that affect a person's mood, might contribute to binge behavior. These studies suggest how eating—or not eating—can actually influence how someone feels mentally. Unhealthy habits can develop as a result.

Cultural messages about beauty

While psychological or biological causes may trigger an eating disorder, behind every disorder is a broader cultural issue. When patients recovering from eating disorders tell their personal stories, they mention their desire to be thin or an obsession with weight. So, how does a person come to believe that a thin body is the ultimate goal?

Society's messages about an ideal body are difficult to ignore. From television and film images to magazine pages, the concept of beauty in American culture has become increasingly tied to thinness. According to one doctor, "For centuries there has been pressure to look a certain way, because one's body is a presentation of who you are to the culture. Now it's to look contoured, perfect. Preteens see the models, they see the advertisements, and they have been around Barbie dolls since they were young. They are bombarded by highly unrealistic ideals."[17]

These powerful messages about thinness as an ideal reach almost everyone in American society, leaving a strong impression especially on children and teenagers. If girls are exposed to the message that a thin body is what they need to strive for, that standard can affect their body image well into the future. As they grow older, the same cultural messages constantly reinforce those ideas about which body types are acceptable.

"I WANT TO BE THIN LIKE ALLY MCBEAL, STACKED LIKE BARBIE and ETERNALLY YOUNG LIKE A SUPERMODEL.... NOW IF YOU'LL EXCUSE ME, I HAVE TO GO VOMIT MY HAPPY MEAL."

Jim Borgman. Reprinted by special permission of King Features Syndicate.

Ideas about body image are often transmitted through the mass media—particularly in television and print advertising. Regardless of the product, advertisements can send unintentional messages about how one should look. In the United States, ads feature female models who are well below the average weight of American women. Bombarded with unrealistic pictures of how their bodies should look, it is not surprising that some girls strive for a physique that is neither achievable nor healthy.

Losing weight becomes a source of pride and accomplishment for a person with anorexia. However, anorexics never feel that they have lost enough weight.

The result is often a state of unhealthy confusion. One doctor explains that girls today "are getting mixed messages. On one hand, they're striving healthfully toward a broad range of access and opportunities. On the other hand, they're being told that to achieve their goals, they must look a certain way. Many girls think that 'normal' isn't good enough."[18] This cultural pressure to look a specific way lays the foundation in some youngsters for an eating disorder.

Good intentions sometimes become obsessions

In spite of the good intentions underlying many attempts at dieting, research has found that about one-third of all diets turn into unhealthy preoccupations. Diets, however, do not *cause* eating disorders; a disorder is rooted in a complex web of psychological, biological, and cultural factors. While dieting is often a part of the picture, other factors must also be present for an eating disorder to develop. For those in whom such factors exist, dieting can spiral out of control into a full-blown eating disorder.

A diet may begin with a short-term goal to lose a few pounds and thereby improve one's confidence and well-being. Yet given other factors in a person's life, that goal can turn into an obsession. It is estimated that about 95 percent of dieters regain their lost weight, and regaining that weight can lead to a greater fixation with weight loss or control.

Self-esteem

Even though an eating disorder involves a person's eating habits, food is not really at the root of the problem. In fact, as one recovering anorexic sums it up, "Eating disorders have nothing to do with food. There is something much deeper going on."[19] An eating disorder, therefore, is often a symptom of other problems. Those who suffer from eating disorders may simply be coping with their problems through self-starvation, bingeing, or purging.

More often than not, low self-esteem is the basis for an eating disorder. One research study analyzed the concerns of adolescents suffering from eating disorders. The researchers surveyed a group of twenty-six anorexics and thirty bulimics. They found that 54 percent of the anorexics and 70 percent of the bulimics expressed concerns related to self-esteem. Having a poor sense of self-worth, a person may use his or her relationship with food or body weight to boost self-esteem.

The idea that controlling or losing weight will somehow remedy other problems can establish a pattern that is difficult to break. In some cases, losing or controlling weight gives the person, at least temporarily, a sense of high self-esteem and he or she will feel compelled to control that weight to maintain some sense of self-worth.

Yet this method of coping does not solve the underlying problems with self-esteem. Instead, such individuals become dependent on the fixation with food or weight loss for feeling "better" about themselves. The obsession becomes intertwined with identity—and it becomes difficult for people with eating disorders to think of themselves aside from what they eat or do not eat.

Self-control

Besides self-esteem, eating disorders appear to be rooted in a need for control. Often those with eating disorders say that focusing intensely on food, weight, or exercise gives them a sense of control in their lives. Perhaps in other aspects of their lives they feel insecure, dissatisfied, or helpless. With weight control, however, they can be fully in charge of their behavior and how it affects their bodies. The obsession with control is more characteristic of anorexics and bulimics than binge eaters, however, since binge eating disorder is characterized by a loss of control.

One recovering anorexic remembers associating weight control with success. When people commented on her extremely thin appearance, she felt a sense of accomplishment: "I took these comments as compliments. I thought these people were jealous of my body, envied me for how much weight I had lost. Their comments reassured me—confirmed that I was doing a good job restricting my calories. I was successful."[20]

Unfortunately, the feeling of having control can become

dangerously addictive. Once an anorexic loses weight or a bulimic purges a day's food consumption, any sense of contentment is brief. The need to lose still more weight or to purge calories in some way often returns.

Ironically, the person trying to remain in charge of food intake or weight may actually be losing control to the eating disorder. As one recovering anorexic describes her eating

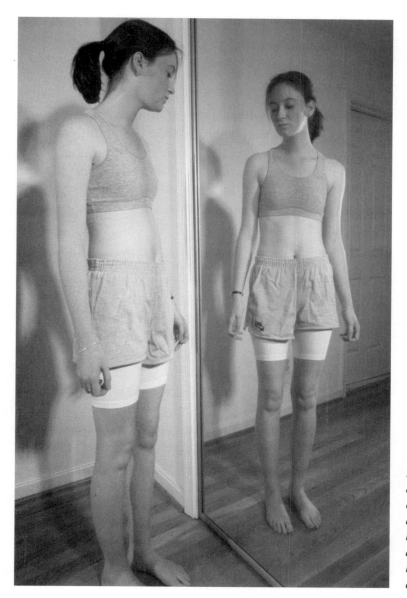

People suffering from an eating disorder often develop a distorted view of their bodies and cannot acknowledge that they have become excessively thin.

behavior, "I often feel that is the only part of my life over which I can exercise any sort of control, though it ends up in the absurdity of feeling that every bit is an act of losing control." [21]

A drive for perfection

Having a perfectionistic personality can also contribute to the obsessive behavior of eating disorders. Perfectionists set very high standards for themselves. One doctor explains, "Eating disorders are most common among high achievers, those who try hardest to conform to our cultural ideas of perfection." [22] Given the high value American society seems to place on being slender, this vulnerability to eating disorders among high achievers is predictable. Many people with eating disorders are driven to succeed and become overachievers in work, school, or other activities. Once they decide to change their body shape, they relentlessly strive to attain that goal, which becomes a priority above everything else.

Coping with emotions

Regardless of the risk factors involved, every eating disorder involves a strong tie between emotions and one's relationship with food. When patients recovering from eating disorders reflect on how their disorders began, many recall that they were lonely, depressed, or under significant stress at the time. In fact, it is estimated that 80 percent of bulimics also suffer from depression.

Specific episodes in a person's life might trigger an episode of disordered eating. For example, when any kind of emotional distress or life transition occurs—such as breaking up with a boyfriend or girlfriend, problems at home with parents or siblings, challenges at school or work, or dealing with the death of a loved one—a person seeks out ways to feel better. Eating habits such as food deprivation, bingeing, or purging can become a crutch for someone dealing with such difficult events. Focusing on one's relationship with food becomes a private method of coping with pain.

Even so, consoling oneself by eating or not eating does

not cure the pain. As one recovering bulimic explains, "If I ate, no matter what it was, it was too much and I had to get it out of my body. . . . There was about five minutes after I purged where I felt a numbness. The pain inside subsided. Only to return stronger shortly thereafter."[23]

Survivors of physical or psychological abuse may also be at risk for developing eating disorders. This is especially true if they have been reluctant to express their feelings concerning what happened to them to their family members or friends. When these problems are not addressed in an upfront way, the survivor might express painful feelings or confusion through disordered eating.

Developing eating habits and body image

Studies have shown that the degree of control that parents exert over what a child eats, as well as when to eat and how much, can affect the child's development of normal, healthy eating habits. Some supervision of a child's eating is necessary, but controlling food intake too much can be counterproductive. Even consistently requiring a child to clean his or her plate at the dinner table can affect later eating behaviors. Experts suggest that children be given some amount of control over their food intake so they will learn about eating to satisfy hunger rather than some arbitrarily imposed amount.

For some victims of physical or psychological abuse, eating disorders are an expression of their pain or confusion.

Eating more than the body needs appears to be a behavior that is learned early. A recent study indicated that by age three or four, a child's eating habits may become influenced by external factors, not simply by hunger. Researchers studied groups of three-year-olds and five-year-olds and found that no matter the size of the portion, the three-year-olds ate only until they were no longer hungry whereas the five-year-olds' eating appeared to be driven by the size of the portions. The study results suggest that external influences, such as the guidance that parents give their children, can affect a person's eating habits.

In addition to eating habits, concern about physical appearance may also be learned at home. Parents may unknowingly make statements that affect how a child views his or her own body. One woman recalls that her body image was influenced by her mother's own body image. At age thirteen, she and her mother were close to the same height, but she weighed fifteen pounds more than her mother. She remembers, "You know what my mom called herself when we were growing up? Godzilla. I weighed more than she did. If she was Godzilla, what was I?"[24]

"I just wanted to fade away"

The impact of family behavior on an eating disorder does not just involve the way someone learns to view food. The anxiety that accompanies family problems such as divorce or alcoholism can trigger behavior leading to an eating disorder, especially if there is a history of poor communication in the family. When family problems occur, focusing on food or weight might become a substitute for communicating openly with family members about whatever is happening in the home.

One nineteen-year-old recovering from an eating disorder recalls, "My parents separated when I was 16, and I never told anybody how bad I felt about it. I pulled away from everyone, dropped out of school, and dieted until I was so thin my mother said I looked like death warmed over. But I didn't care. It sounds awful, but I just wanted to fade away and disappear. That way I'd be safe."[25]

For some, behavior like starving, bingeing, or purging might seem soothing amid family stress, even though it is physically unhealthy. It becomes a private escape from the realities of an upsetting home life—and because it seems like a refuge, one does not recognize that the eating disorder is damaging in itself.

One eating disorder specialist emphasizes, however, that

family difficulties like illness or divorce should not be viewed as primary causes of eating disorders. Instead, they are triggers that can bring on an eating disorder in someone who is already at risk. Peggy Claude-Pierre, founder of the Montreux Clinic, explains, "If a child is already feeling negative . . . about what is going on in her life, she is more vulnerable . . . to taking these emergencies personally and feeling helpless about them." If a person is more affected by these "pessimistic thought patterns—that is, if they dominate 60 percent of her thoughts rather than 20 percent—the more effective the trigger will be in setting off the eating disorder."[26]

Eating disorders develop for a variety of reasons, however, and it should be noted that while some may be partially triggered by family problems, such disorders can also occur in what appear to be trouble-free homes. It is possible that in a loving, nurturing home environment, an eating disorder could still develop as a result of other psychological, biological, or cultural factors. Moreover, risk factors, causes, and triggers can vary depending on the disorder. In fact, in one study, 40 percent of bulimic adolescents expressed concerns about family rapport but only 15 per-

Family problems can contribute to the development of an eating disorder.

cent of anorexic teens indicated similar concerns.

Gender issues

Of those who struggle with eating disorders, about 90 percent are girls and women. Males and females obviously have an equal need for food as a source of nourishment and good health, so why are girls and women more vulnerable to eating disorders than boys and men?

Traditionally, society has placed a greater importance on physical appearance for girls and women. Studies have shown that girls and women are more prone to being dissatisfied with their bodies and are more likely to initiate a diet or exercise program in order to correct what they perceive as a problem.

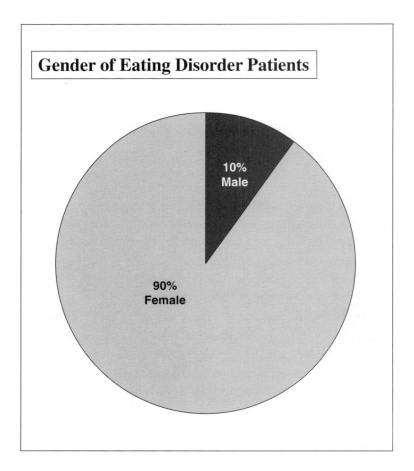

Gender of Eating Disorder Patients

10%
Male

90%
Female

For girls and women, physical appearance seems to affect their overall sense of well-being more than it does for boys and men. In one survey of men who were clinically considered overweight, "Even men who are 200 pounds overweight by conventional standards . . . [said] that being fat wasn't very important in their lives; they seemed not to think about it very much and claimed it didn't cause them suffering in work or in their personal relationships." [27]

In terms of self-perceptions, males and females also tend to assess their bodies differently. In a study concerning adolescents' self-image during puberty, researchers analyzed how girls and boys perceived their bodies. When asked what they liked best and least about their bodies, girls mentioned facial features, legs, and hips as being concerns. Boys, on the other hand, most often noted athletic abilities as their primary concern. The study also found that "perception of and satisfaction with weight are important variables for girls. They are more important for a girl's body image than they are for a boy's." [28]

Although males tend to focus less on weight management than females, the number of males affected by eating disorders has risen sharply in recent years.

In American culture, males and females receive different kinds of messages about what is a desirable body. Females are under the impression that a thin, lean body is ideal, and they may feel pressure to meet society's standards of thinness. In contrast, the male ideal is that of a built-up, muscle-toned body. As a result, males tend to focus less on weight management than females do.

The psychological risk factors leading to eating disorders—such as low self-esteem, depression, and family problems—can apply to both females and males. Like females, males who diet in their adolescent and early adult years are especially vulnerable to developing eating disorders. The Center for Eating Disorders notes, however, that men may experience certain risk factors more often than women. These factors include having been obese and teased about their weight as well as pursuing weight loss in association with athletic activities.

In recent years, the number of males affected by eating disorders has increased. At one time, about one boy experienced an eating disorder for every nineteen girls. Now that gap has closed significantly, and the ratio has moved closer to one boy for every eight or nine girls. That change may be the result of an increasing emphasis on physical appearance among men in American society. More than ever, males and females alike appear to be feeling the pressure to be thin.

Age and body image

Eating disorders can occur in both women and men, and they can affect people at any age. However, just as statistics indicate that the majority of those with eating disorders are girls and women, there are also trends in the ages of those affected by this illness. According to the American Anorexia Bulimia Association (AABA), anorexia most frequently develops at age twelve or thirteen and at age seventeen. Bulimia most commonly develops in the late teen years and in the early twenties, though it can develop at a younger age. Statistics indicate that, unlike other eating disorders, binge eating disorder does not affect any particular age group disproportionately.

The prevalence of anorexia and bulimia among teenagers suggests that they are particularly vulnerable to these eating disorders. There are reasons for this. As early teenagers go through puberty, they experience significant body changes. For many teenagers, watching their bodies change can stir a mix of different emotions and concerns. The fact that adolescent bodies develop at widely different rates during puberty—some slower or faster than others—leads some teenagers to become self-conscious about their bodies in comparison to those of their peers.

At the same time, the teenage years usually bring new social pressures. Feelings of insecurity are common as some teens struggle for social acceptance. During these years, teenagers often observe their peers to get a sense of how they should act—or how they should look.

The combination of concerns about their own development and about being accepted by their peers can put teens at particular risk of developing eating disorders. One recovering anorexic recalls her experience during high school:

> When I went to high school, chronologically younger than many of my classmates, and still younger developmentally, I saw that many of the girls in the locker room had figures already. I reasoned that the only way to have a thin waist like theirs was by dieting—if my plump middle got smaller, and the top and the bottom got added to, or just stayed the same, then I'd look more like the other girls did. Also, I thought that boys were noticing me. Their attention made me feel awkward and terribly embarrassed. I imagined that if I could lose weight from all the bad places and put it on in all the right ones, then maybe I would look like I fit in better, and I wouldn't feel so out of place." [29]

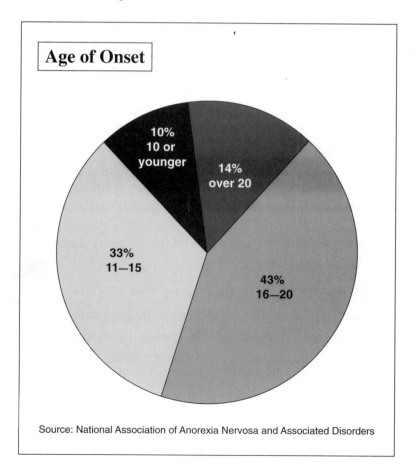

Age of Onset

10% 10 or younger

14% over 20

33% 11—15

43% 16—20

Source: National Association of Anorexia Nervosa and Associated Disorders

Some therapists who treat eating disorders believe that for girls going through puberty, the natural body changes can result in a subconscious fear of growing up. As girls experience changes such as the onset of menstrual periods or the natural filling-out of their figures, some feel self-conscious or insecure. According to this line of reasoning, some girls wish that they could maintain the familiar body shape of their childhood and by doing so hang on to the security of childhood as well. As one recovering anorexic describes it, "Fearing the physical changes that accompany puberty, the anorexic girl strives for control, trying to whittle her body back into childhood." [30]

"Food is one thing they can control"

Although young adolescents are at risk, college students are also vulnerable. In a recent poll of 460 college health officials, 70 percent of them called eating disorders a "common" problem on their campuses. The organization Eating Disorders Awareness and Prevention (EDAP) states that anywhere from 5 to 7 percent of American undergraduates suffer from anorexia, bulimia, or binge eating disorder.

For many college students, leaving home may be an exciting adventure of newfound independence. Yet the experience may cause others to struggle with feelings of loneliness or insecurity. Jennifer Biely, director of EDAP, says, "College women are away from their families, and there's tremendous pressure to find their way in the world. Food is one thing they can control." [31]

Athletes and eating disorders

If girls in their early teens and college-age women are at particular risk of developing eating disorders, so are athletes, both male and female. In fact, as a group, athletes are especially vulnerable. According to the group Anorexia Nervosa and Related Eating Disorders, "Several studies suggest that participants in sports that emphasize appearance and a lean body are at higher risk for developing an eating disorder than are non-athletes." [32]

One study of male and female athletes determined that one-third of the athletes expressed a preoccupation with food. The study also found that about one-fourth of the group had binge eating episodes at least once a week. Likewise, 15 percent of the athletes had distorted body images, perceiving themselves to be overweight when in reality they were not.

Athletic activities place an emphasis on having a body that is physically fit. Moreover, in addition to a low body-fat percentage, some sports, by their very nature, impose specific body weights or sizes. Despite whether an instructor or coach verbally conveys these physical requirements, many athletes place pressure on themselves to meet certain physical standards. As one coach describes wrestlers, "The instilled attitude among these kids is that if they push and push, it'll pay off with a victory."[33]

Sometimes that push to excel goes too far. When athletes or coaches associate being competitive with having a particular body condition, eating and exercise habits can become obsessive, which can lead to eating disorders. Says one high school gymnast struggling with bulimia, "I blame my training for my eating disorder. Our coach has weekly weigh-ins where we count each others' ribs. If they are hard to count we're in trouble."[34]

The focus among athletes on minimizing body fat can lead to unhealthy regimens of diet and exercise.

The risk of a disorder is greater for athletic activities that require a trim body, so runners, swimmers, and gymnasts are particularly vulnerable. Wrestlers are at risk because they frequently fast in order to qualify for a particular weight class. In addition to fasting, other temporary weight-loss techniques like purging and excessive exercise can become so much a part of the athlete's routine that they can contribute to the development of an eating disorder.

Biological factors

For a long time, researchers looked at eating disorders as mainly a psychological illness. However, recent research has focused also on the possible role of biochemical processes in eating disorders. One angle has examined the relationship between eating disorders and serotonin, a chemical produced in the brain when a person eats. Serotonin affects a person's mood, whether he or she feels happy or depressed, calm or anxious.

Studies on both bulimia and binge eating have explored whether serotonin levels in the brain may be linked to binge behavior. When a person eats, especially high-carbohydrate foods, the chemical process that leads to the brain's production of serotonin speeds up, which in turn causes mood elevations. Because serotonin levels tend to rise after an eating binge, overeaters come to associate their behavior with emotional comfort.

In the case of bulimics, if the binge is followed by a period of purging, serotonin levels will drop again, causing further depression, and the chemical reaction becomes a cycle of ups and downs. (Ironically, anorexics who starve themselves in the belief that not eating will make them feel better may actually be causing a biochemical reaction that prevents them from feeling happy.)

Research into the biological causes of eating disorders is ongoing. Some studies are even exploring the possibility that some people may be genetically prone to developing eating disorders. Doctors studying possible biological causes for eating disorders hope that, in some cases, more effective medical treatments for the illnesses might be found.

3

The Effects of Eating Disorders

EVERY EATING DISORDER is harmful to the body. Whether a person struggles from anorexia, bulimia, binge eating disorder, or a borderline disorder, the physical effects are potentially dangerous. And as an eating disorder intensifies, the health consequences become increasingly severe. Despite the gravity of the consequences, however, one common feature of eating disorders is that their physical symptoms may not become obvious to family and friends until the victim's health has already begun to deteriorate to dangerous levels.

The effects of anorexia: Starving the body

Because anorexia is a form of self-starvation, the body reacts to the condition in predictable ways: Like any malnourished person, an anorexic experiences weakness, dizziness, and possibly even fainting. For an anorexic who exercises excessively, the physical impact is even worse. The body is already in a weakened condition from inadequate food intake, and pushing oneself in an effort to burn more calories places an added strain on the malnourished body, especially when other anorexia-related health conditions exist.

One of the physical strains experienced by anorexics is a sensitivity to coldness. Since anorexics have lost a significant amount of fat, they lack the natural layer of insulation that the human body requires for comfort. For an anorexic, a temperature that would feel warm to other people can feel quite cold. Anorexics also find that moving from cold environments to warm ones can be uncomfortable.

But the sensitivity to coldness goes beyond discomfort. In a desperate attempt to maintain its temperature, an anorexic's body produces a thin layer of hair, known as lanugo. Lanugo, which has a fine, soft appearance, may begin to grow on the face, neck, torso, arms, or legs. This layer of hair is the body's way of protecting itself and of surviving under particularly adverse conditions.

Because the human body requires fat to manufacture essential oils, an anorexic's skin, nails, and hair become dry. As hair becomes thin and brittle, it can break or fall out completely. According to the authors of *Dying to Be Thin*, "No matter if your hair is strong or weak, shiny or dull, oily or dry, it will start to break and fall out if you starve yourself. . . . The only way to make your hair bounce back into shape is to nourish your body with the food it needs first to survive, and then to thrive."[35]

An anorexic's skin may also be a sign that something is wrong. Due to malnutrition, the skin can take on a yellow tone that is visibly different from its normal color. The discoloration results from a condition called hypercarotenemia. The exact cause of this condition is unknown, but it exists in the majority of anorexia patients.

Virtually every bodily function is affected by anorexia. For women and postpubescent girls, when the body's fat levels are significantly lower than normal, menstrual periods become irregular. For some anorexics, these effects may appear even before they have lost a substantial amount of weight. Over time, menstruation can stop altogether.

The long-term health consequences of anorexia

Even as anorexics literally starve their bodies, their own physical symptoms may not alert them to the health dangers. Obsessed with weight loss, many anorexics refuse to acknowledge the deterioration of their own health. As one recovering anorexic says, "I was exhausted all the time. My period stopped for four months, my hair was thinning. But I never connected it with not eating."[36] Yet with the body's vital functions weakened, even more serious medical complications arise.

The malnourishment eventually takes its toll on an anorexic's bones. Osteoporosis, a disorder characterized by a decrease in bone density, is usually experienced by the elderly, but anorexics of any age are at risk of developing the disorder. When osteoporosis develops, bones become dry and fragile and therefore can fracture easily. Osteoporosis is a particular concern for athletes who have eating disorders. If their bones are fragile, then they are at risk of fractures while participating in the normal course of sports activities.

Osteoporosis is not only serious but also sometimes permanent. Although osteoporosis can be treated with hormone replacement therapy and with calcium and vitamin D supplements, recovering from anorexia does not always fully heal the bones. According to one research study, osteoporosis is not necessarily reversible when an anorexic begins to eat normally again. The researchers note that "there are indications that bone density may never attain normal levels, leaving individuals at risk for serious osteoporosis later in life."[37]

The Physical Dangers of Anorexia

▶ Irregular heartbeat

▶ In females, lack of menstrual periods

▶ Dehydration, kidney stones, or kidney failure

▶ Lanugo, or fine body hair that develops to keep body warm

▶ Muscle atrophy

▶ Bowel irritation and constipation

▶ Osteoporosis as a result of calcium loss

Source: National Eating Disorders Organization

Other effects of anorexia are literally life-threatening. Anorexia places a major strain on the heart. The disorder affects the body's normal potassium and sodium levels, which creates what is called an electrolyte imbalance. Electrolytes are essential for the body's muscles and nerves to function properly. An electrolyte imbalance can result in an irregular heartbeat, known as cardiac arrhythmia, and possible heart failure. Anorexia also slows metabolism and lowers a person's blood pressure. In addition, body organs can shrink, and severe dehydration may cause damage to the kidneys, putting the anorexic at risk of kidney failure. Tragically, the most severe cases of anorexia result in death. Although many anorexics are able to fully recover from the disorder with treatment, nearly 15 percent of all anorexics die as a result of the physical effects of starvation.

The behavioral warning signs of anorexia

In spite of the potentially devastating effects of anorexia, even close friends and family members may fail to detect the problem early on, since the anorexic's behavior is often kept hidden from view. However, it is likely that a person with an eating disorder will begin to leave a trail of clues. As the eating disorder intensifies with time, it becomes harder for a person to hide abnormal behavior from others.

If their anorexic behavior is not detected, the physical symptoms of anorexia serve as a warning that an individual needs immediate medical attention. Although any one behavior does not necessarily mean that a disorder exists, it is when several—or all—of these typical patterns are apparent that suggests anorexia might have developed. Warning signs include a significant loss of weight—particularly when the person does not have a known medical illness—as well as a noticeable decrease in food consumption. When offered food or invited to share in a meal, anorexics may repeatedly respond that they are not hungry. When they do eat, they may show signs of having eating rituals, like cutting up food in a particular way or taking a long time to chew each bite. They are also likely to eat strictly

Warning Signs of Anorexia

▶ Significant weight loss

▶ Continuing to diet (although thin)

▶ Distorted body image (feeling fat even when thin)

▶ Fear of weight gain

▶ In females, lack of menstrual periods

▶ Preoccupation with food, calories, nutrition, and/or cooking

▶ Preferring to exercise alone

▶ Compulsive exercising

▶ Bingeing and purging

Source: American Anorexia Bulimia Association, Inc.

low-fat or low-calorie foods and may express the belief that any other foods are "bad" or "wrong."

Aside from their eating habits, anorexics might also show signs of overexercise or overactivity. Anorexics usually follow an exercise routine in a rigid, obsessive manner. It is more likely to be a solitary form of exercise—like jogging or working out at a gym—as opposed to a group activity. In addition to this deliberate form of overexercise, anorexics may also show signs of a general restlessness, which can be the body's reaction to food deprivation. For some anorexics, the restlessness can even lead to insomnia.

Anorexics often become judgmental of others and behave as if they feel alienated, tending to isolate themselves from family and friends. They are usually disciplined in their behavior—not just in how they eat or exercise—but also in how they deal with other aspects of daily life, such as school, work, or other activities.

Anorexics will also indicate signs of a poor body image. They may complain of being overweight—even when it is not true—or make statements suggesting that they do not perceive themselves realistically. And they may act overly self-conscious about physical appearance in general.

A strain on the digestive system

Bulimics suffer from some of the same physical effects as anorexics, yet other consequences are uniquely the result of the repeated bingeing and purging. Similar to anorexics, bulimics commonly feel the weakness and fatigue that are the outward signs of poor nutrition. Because of the constant purging, they are often dehydrated and experience dry skin as a result.

Also like anorexics, bulimics experience low potassium and sodium levels in the body due to their purging behavior. As with anorexics, the electrolyte imbalance puts them at risk of heart failure. For girls and women with bulimia, irregular periods may occur. And because they lack proper nutrition, bulimics are also at risk of osteoporosis.

Bulimia, however, carries with it some distinct medical consequences that are the result of the cycles of bingeing and purging. Bingeing, for example, is stressful to the digestive system, which is not used to coping with such a rapid consumption of large food portions. The frequent practice of self-induced vomiting leads bulimics to experience a sore throat and swollen salivary glands, which can appear visibly puffy in the face and neck. Bulimics may also experience constipation, irregular bowel movements, and indigestion.

In addition, stomach acids brought up during vomiting eat into tooth enamel, leading to decay. A bulimic's teeth may be visibly gray. As one dentist explains, "The stomach acid erodes the hard enamel that protects the dentin, which is the softer inner material of the tooth. If the dentin is exposed and left unprotected, the teeth undergo accelerated wear and are particularly vulnerable to decay. In other words, without extensive capping, bulimia can destroy a beautiful smile."[38]

Purging by vomiting also irritates the esophagus, the tube that leads from the mouth to the stomach. Food passes through the esophagus during digestion. The esophagus is not ordinarily exposed to the stomach's acids, so it becomes inflamed from frequent vomiting. Eventually, weakened by the constant exposure to acid, the esophagus can rupture.

Vomiting is not the only form of purging with dangerous side effects, however. Laxative abuse also has serious health consequences. Laxative abuse results in abnormal bowel function, as the colon stops responding to the body's natural signals. But even before this happens, overuse of laxatives leads to a variety of unpleasant side effects, such as stomach pains, diarrhea, nausea, or constipation. Other long-term side effects of laxative abuse can include irregular heartbeat (caused by the electrolyte imbalance that results from low potassium and sodium levels in the body), urinary tract infections, and kidney failure (due to dehydration).

Damaging vital organs

A bulimic's frequent vomiting is problematic in its own right, but the means that some bulimics use to induce vomiting can also cause problems. The active ingredient in one purgative, ipecac, is called emetine. The body gets rid of emetine through the kidneys, an elimination process that can take as long as two months. During that time, the body stores emetine in muscle tissue. Regular ipecac users may feel weakness, aching, or stiffness of muscles. But these side effects are particularly serious since they can occur in any muscle, including the intestines, stomach, diaphragm, or even the heart. The result can be diarrhea, stomach cramps, difficulty in breathing, and irregular heartbeat. And because this damage to the heart can be irreversible, death due to cardiac arrest is a very real threat.

Bulimics can fully recover from their disorder, but it is possible that their digestive systems can suffer from permanent damage in the meantime. Long-term physical effects of bulimia include damage to the liver, kidney, and bowels; peptic ulcers; and pancreatitis, or inflammation of the pancreas. Bulimics may experience vomiting of blood and severe stomach cramps. With the strain on the digestive system, bulimics also risk the possibility of rupturing their stomachs during bingeing.

The behavioral warning signs of bulimia

While the physical symptoms of anorexia are usually the most obvious to others at the advanced stages of the disorder, the warning signs of bulimia may be easier to detect because bulimics often leave behind indications of their unusual purging behavior. As one doctor explains, "Bulimics will often leave evidence around—laxatives on the dresser, vomitus in the toilet bowl—as if they want to get caught."[39] For people close to a bulimic, some physical symptoms might suggest that there is a problem, but behavioral patterns can also be an alert. As with anorexia, there is usually a combination of some or all of these warning signs when bulimia exists.

The way in which a bulimic relates to food is a key warning sign. The bulimic may purchase very large

---

Warning Signs of Bulimia

▶ Frequent bingeing or eating uncontrollably

▶ Purging after a binge by fasting, excessive exercise, vomiting, or abusing laxatives or diuretics

▶ Using the bathroom frequently after meals

▶ Preoccupation with body weight

▶ Depression or mood swings

▶ Irregular menstrual periods

▶ Development of dental problems, swollen cheeks/ glands, heartburn and/or bloating

▶ Experiencing personal or family problems with drugs or alcohol

Source: American Anorexia Bulimia Association, Inc.

amounts of food at a time, and afterward the food seems to be gone quickly. Food might be mysteriously missing from the person's home or from a shared kitchen, as in a college dormitory or other communal space. Although bulimics usually binge in privacy, there may still be occasions when they are seen eating unusually big portions quickly.

There can also be clues pointing to the purging habits of a bulimic. Bulimics may disappear after meals—the time when they purge food in private—or, if they are around people, they may frequently offer reasons for having to go to the bathroom after they eat. And if bulimics use laxatives or diuretics as purging methods, they will inevitably throw away wrappers from these products in the trash can, leaving evidence of a problem.

Bulimics' mood changes are also warning signs. Because bulimics' mental state is so related to where they are in the binge-purge cycle, frequent mood changes can occur. They appear depressed after a binge but then display a somewhat elevated mood after a purge—and they continue on that cycle. Like anorexics, bulimics usually also show signs of being overly conscious of body image or general physical appearance.

The health risks of binge eating disorder

Since those who suffer from binge eating disorder do not try to purge their bodies of the food they have eaten, the main consequence of binge eating disorder is obesity. The potential effects of binge eating disorder on one's health, therefore, are the physical dangers associated with obesity, including heart disease and high blood pressure. Because obesity affects the normal functioning of the gallbladder and increases the risk of gallstones, gallbladder disease is a potential problem for binge eaters. The risk of stroke or heart attack, as well as the risk of breast, reproductive, and bowel cancers, has also been found to be higher among those who are obese.

In addition, secondary diabetes is associated with obesity, so binge eaters are at risk of that malady. Fat hinders the functioning of insulin, which the body needs to metabolize

Medical Consequences of Binge Eating Disorder	
certain types of cancer	heart disease
diabetes	high blood pressure
gall bladder disease	high cholesterol
Source: American Anorexia Bulimia Association, Inc.	

sugar properly. For a person of a healthy weight, a normal amount of body fat does not prevent insulin from doing its job. But for an obese person, insulin cannot function properly, so the sugar stays in the blood instead of getting to the cells. This causes high levels of blood sugar, which can lead to diabetes.

The psychological effects of eating disorders

Just as the physical effects of eating disorders are serious, so too are the psychological ones. Low self-esteem and depression are often underlying causes of anorexia, bulimia, and binge eating disorder, and some people with eating disorders believe that their behavior will help to lift their feelings of despair. But ironically, their eating habits are more likely to worsen their depression because they are unable to feel good about themselves outside of their relationship with food or their body image. As one doctor describes some of her anorexia patients, "All had given up on life. They didn't expect to have fun or to find human interaction rewarding. Their lives had become relentless, grim encounters with scales and calorie charts."[40] That is the difficult trap of eating disorders: The negative feelings that cause a disorder usually just intensify as the abnormal behavior continues. In other words, a person with an eating disorder is likely to continue feeling depressed as long as the unhealthy eating patterns continue.

This vicious cycle is intensified by feelings of isolation. As an eating disorder progresses, sufferers begin to feel that they cannot relate to friends or family, and it becomes harder to communicate openly with others. One person recovering from anorexia and bulimia recalls,

> The more I got into the dieting, and later on the more I binged and threw up, the less I cared about other things or people. . . . I actually forgot how to have fun with friends. . . . The longer I did my thing, the more I felt like I was moving around in a fog—a blanketing fog that could shield me from everyone and everything I used to want to be around."[41]

Moreover, because they do not want anyone to interfere with their eating habits, many who suffer from eating disorders become more and more isolated.

Inevitably, the private obsession with food and weight becomes more intense with time and it becomes difficult to think of anything else. Randi E. Wirth, executive director of the American Anorexia Bulimia Association, says, "Eating disorders are a 24-hour-a-day fixation. They are with you from the moment you awake to the moment you fall asleep. Counting those calories, fear of getting fat—that's all you think about."[42] The only way out is to seek help, get professional treatment and support, and begin a course toward recovery.

4

Treating
Eating Disorders

DESPITE THE SERIOUS dangers to their health, it is difficult for those with eating disorders to recognize that their behavior is harmful and requires treatment. Even when anorexics, bulimics, or binge eaters begin experiencing major medical problems, they may deny that any connection exists between their poor health and their eating habits. They may still find ways to rationalize their abnormal eating habits. If they do not seek help on their own, intervention by someone else is the first step toward treatment.

Intervention

Initially the biggest hurdle in treating an eating disorder is getting the person to face the fact that a problem really exists. Those who can acknowledge their illness and seek help on their own have already taken the first step in the healing process. But the majority of people with eating disorders have trouble facing the problem on their own. In such cases, family or friends can help in confronting the problem and in obtaining professional help.

Approaching a person about his or her eating disorder is difficult, however, since speaking openly about the problem is usually a challenge for the person struggling with the illness. The conversation is likely to stir up many feelings that could be difficult to express. Some people may find that it is a relief to finally talk about how they have been feeling; meanwhile, others may be defensive and resist the offer of help. The American Anorexia Bulimia Association advises,

> When you address the problem initially, you need to prepare yourself for all possible reactions. The person you are confronting may become upset, defensive, and/or angry. There is also a chance that s/he will be relieved that someone has offered to help. Either way, you need to stress the fact that you are bringing the issue up because you care about the person, and that you are genuinely concerned about her/his well-being." [43]

Even when family or friends offer help, however, the person still may be resistant. Few people with eating disorders have the sense of control and perspective to admit to themselves that their habits are harmful and need to change; they are too wrapped up in thoughts about food, weight, or body shape. And while some may be able to acknowledge that their behavior is unusual, they might still lack the ability to confront the disorder and assess how it is affecting them physically and psychologically. Of all the eating disorders, studies have shown that anorexics are

WATERLOO HIGH SCHOOL LIBRARY
1464 INDUSTRY RD.
ATWATER, OH 44201

Although people with eating disorders are often resistant to treatment, family members find that their support can make a difference in a person's recovery.

least aware that their attitude toward food is unhealthy; therefore, they also may be more resistant to treatment.

Facing the problem

Yet it is unlikely that an eating disorder will just run its course and taper off with time. As one doctor explains, "Very rarely do I hear someone say, 'Oh yes, I had bulimia for three years and I just stopped one day and now I'm fine.' It's very hard to give up the behavior. Once somebody tells me they've done this several times—in my mind, they're probably hooked."[44] Recovery usually requires some form of treatment.

The idea of professional treatment may seem overwhelming to a person suffering from an eating disorder. If others offer assistance in that process—whether researching treatment options or accompanying him or her to see a counselor, for example—it helps to lift some of the burden off the person with the disorder. For such people, it may be stressful enough just admitting their problem to themselves and to their friends and family, and seeking professional help may be a step they are unwilling to take.

Once a person with an eating disorder does agree to seek help, a range of treatment options is available. In order to determine which option is best, treatment begins by assessing the patient's needs and designing a treatment program that meets those needs.

While there are various therapies available, the common goal of eating disorder treatment is to restore a positive body image and a healthy relationship with food. That can include evaluating the underlying reasons for negative body image or unhealthy eating—and then thinking about how to change one's responses to those factors.

Recovery also involves boosting self-esteem and regaining a sense of control in one's life. Treatment can help those with eating disorders to regain control of their behavior, to make healthy choices for themselves, and to break the tie they have created between self-esteem and food or weight. Moving toward full recovery can be a long process; depending on the individual, it could take several

Treatment	
Treatment for people with eating disorders may include:	
Hospitalization	to prevent death, suicide, and medical crisis
Medication	to relieve depression and anxiety
Dental work	to repair damage and minimize future problems
Individual counseling	to develop healthy ways of taking control
Group counseling	to learn how to manage relationships effectively
Family counseling	to change old patterns and create healthier new ones
Nutrition counseling	to debunk food myths and design healthy meals
Support groups	to break down isolation and alienation
Source: Anorexia Nervosa and Related Eating Disorders, Inc.	

months or even years. Finding the right treatment setting ensures that a person will receive adequate support and guidance during that process of healing.

Individual therapy

Because eating disorders are thought to be primarily psychological, treatment usually begins with some form of psychotherapy. This first step could consist of one-on-one counseling, family counseling, group counseling, or a combination of these treatments.

For any kind of counseling, the key to success is selecting a therapist with whom a comfortable, trusting relationship can be built. One psychotherapist relates how he gets his eating disorder patients to depend on him so that they can ultimately learn how to trust the people around them. "I make them trust me," he says. "I act as their anchor."[45]

Individual therapy addresses a person's eating habits as well as the underlying causes of the behavior. Therapy

examines issues such as low self-esteem, distorted body image, personal or family problems, and cultural factors that might be at work. The therapist helps the person to acknowledge that he or she has a problem and to understand why it developed. Patients learn to express themselves in healthier ways, not through the vehicle of food. Therapy may also focus on the goal of behavioral changes, so that healthy eating habits can be restored.

The techniques used by therapists vary widely, so even if one therapist is unable to help, another might have greater success. There are several approaches to therapy; two common types include psychodynamic therapy and cognitive-behavioral therapy.

Facing up to the past

Psychodynamic therapy is an approach that revolves around the assumption that past experiences or conflicts might be affecting the patient's current behavior. For eating disorder patients, the process of psychodynamic therapy means looking beyond just the fact that their obsessive behavior is unhealthy. The goal is to gain insight into the other issues behind that behavior—specifically how those issues developed over a person's life—and to attempt to resolve them.

Usually the focus is on a person's childhood years as well as family relationships and dynamics. The therapy also assumes that motives for a person's behavior are often hidden even from the patient. The therapist helps the patient to interpret exactly what those motives are.

Facing the behavior directly

While the psychodynamic approach addresses how thoughts and beliefs are shaped over the course of a person's life, the cognitive-behavioral approach concentrates more on details of present behavior. Cognitive-behavorial therapy analyzes how the patient adapts his or her behavior in response to external factors, such as personal relationships, family roles, work or school environments, and emotions.

This type of counseling explores the factors that trigger the eating disorder and analyzes how the patient reacts to them. That helps the patient to then focus on unraveling unhealthy habits—in a sense, to "unlearn" the pattern of behavior that they have developed in response to relationships or experiences—and restore healthy behavior.

Cognitive-behavioral therapists believe that people develop behaviors partly through reinforcement. If a person receives positive responses after behaving in a certain manner, then they will repeat that behavior. In the view of cognitive-behavioral therapists, a person with an eating disorder gets some sort of positive reaction to some aspect of the eating disorder. For an anorexic or bulimic, this might be praise for losing weight; for someone with binge eating disorder, this might be the feeling of comfort that comes with eating a large amount of food.

Cognitive-behavioral therapists try to change a patient's behavior by adjusting his or her responses to external stimuli. Methods for doing so vary from one therapist to another. Usually the therapist helps the patient focus on what situations prompt specific thoughts or behaviors on a daily basis—and then gradually change that behavior so that unhealthy responses to these same situations are replaced by healthy ones. For example, an anorexic who associates weight loss with achievement would be taught to seek that sense of attainment in more appropriate arenas.

Alternative therapies

Treatment is not limited to traditional methods like psychodynamic and cognitive-behavioral therapy, however. A number of alternative programs exist, such as experiential therapies, which usually either follow or coincide with medical treatment. Therapeutic methods and settings vary, but the long-term goals of experiential therapies are similar to those of traditional therapies.

If patients in traditional therapy do not respond to a specific treatment approach, alternative therapies may provide settings that can better facilitate recovery. For example, some patients may find alternative settings less threatening than the environments or methods of traditional therapists, and a particular environment may help them to be more open to the treatment process.

One example of experiential therapy is known as art therapy, in which participants explore feelings through artistic expression. Another kind is wilderness therapy, in which participants learn about self-confidence, communication, and problem-solving skills through outdoor experiences.

According to the Anorexia Nervosa and Bulimia Association (ANAB), a Canadian-based organization, experiential therapies

> engage learners in the process of their learning and healing. . . . [They are] effective ways of bringing about change in individuals with eating disorders and body image issues because they demand that participants are engaged intellectually, creatively, emotionally/expressively, or physically. This engagement helps [them] look carefully . . . at the places they have been in their lives that bring them to how they are coping right now.[46]

Family therapy

Whatever technique a therapist uses, it can be very beneficial when a family gets involved in treatment. A family's presence can be a vital source of support, helping the patient feel less isolated. In addition, when family mem-

bers participate in therapy, they can sometimes provide insight into any family dynamics underlying the eating disorder. When family therapy is initiated, it may include parents, siblings, the patient's spouse or partner, or some combination of these parties.

Because many eating disorders partially stem from certain family relationships or dynamics, family therapy helps the person suffering from an eating disorder to address these issues with those who have shared the same experiences. The therapist can guide communication among family members about whatever problems or behavioral patterns may have contributed to the eating disorder. Positioned to view matters objectively, the therapist can assist a family in bringing the problems to the surface and addressing them.

Art therapy, in which feelings are explored and expressed, is often used to treat individuals with an eating disorder.

Group therapy

Although many people are helped by intensive one-on-one therapy, some seeking help with eating disorders may find it helpful to undergo therapy with others who are similarly afflicted. Group therapy provides that opportunity. The setting allows participants to explore the causes of their eating disorders—and the emotions associated with

Group therapy offers participants an opportunity to speak openly about their eating disorders with people who can relate to what they are going through.

them—while receiving support from others in the group. Since most people with eating disorders feel isolated from the rest of society by their illnesses, group therapy offers patients a chance to feel more comfortable with others who can relate to what they are experiencing. As one doctor explains, this adds a dimension that is otherwise missing from individual or family therapy:

> Members of psychotherapy groups quickly learn that they can't be as devious with one another as they can with their parents or even with their private therapist. Everyone there knows all the dodges and lies. They learn that they can confront one another and be confronted without feeling either rejected or devastated. This discovery makes honest friendship possible, and close ties often develop between group members. The ability to make close friends, in turn, makes each person feel better about herself.[47]

Support groups

While group therapy is facilitated by a licensed therapist and can be expensive for participants, support groups that are not necessarily led by a licensed professional are often free or low-cost. Support groups provide nurturing environments for people with eating disorders. Whereas group therapy revolves around an analysis of the psychological and behavioral aspects of eating disorders, support groups focus on building a support network and sharing personal stories or advice with those who are also in recovery. Participants discuss the challenges of recovering from eating disorders, and the mutual support helps reduce feelings of isolation during the process of healing.

Support groups are usually not an alternative to therapy; rather, they are an additional resource available to a patient. A person could participate in a support group in conjunction with individual, family, or group therapy. Even after their therapy has ended, some people continue to attend support groups to maintain healthy behavior. In some cases, the support from other sufferers may even help prevent relapses into disordered eating.

Overeaters Anonymous (OA) is one example of a support group for binge eaters. The group is modeled on the twelve-step recovery program for which Alcoholics Anonymous is famous. Reflecting the belief that binge eating is an addictive behavior similar to alcoholism, participants carefully follow a sequence of twelve steps to break away from that addiction. The first step of the program is to own up to the grip that food has on the binge eater: "We admitted we were powerless over food—that our lives had become unmanageable."[48]

Open communication as a tool

OA groups do not have regular leaders, although the meeting discussions are considered confidential. This informal but private atmosphere encourages open communication among participants about their feelings. Members of OA often discuss the issue of personal control, not only in relation to binge eating but also how it applies to their lives in general. They share advice, offer support, and help each other to follow eating plans that can lessen the tendency to binge.

In addition to support groups for binge eaters, there are various support groups available around the country for anorexics and bulimics as well. The groups may include a range of people in recovery, from those initially seeking help to those who have been progressing through treatment for years.

While eating disorder support groups are available for those suffering from these illnesses, family members may also find it helpful to join support groups. Participants can share feelings about helping their loved ones deal with their illnesses, discuss how the struggle has affected their families, and offer advice to one another about treatment and recovery. In turn, they may find that they can provide better support to the family member with the eating disorder.

Nutritional counseling

While therapies focus on the psychological and behavioral roots of an eating disorder and support groups enable those who suffer to bond with others in a similar situation, treatment also involves recreating a healthy relationship with food. That means recognizing its nutritional value for the body.

Nutritional counseling assists a person with an eating disorder to get back on the track of healthy eating by educating the patient about what the body needs to remain strong and function normally. Nutritional counseling is not a substitute for therapy, so it is generally recommended in addition to individual or group therapy. A counseling session—or multiple sessions—with a nutritionist can complement therapy of other kinds.

A nutritionist examines an individual's routine food intake to determine how the diet lacks nutritional balance. The nutritionist may also analyze patterns in weight loss or gain, as well as how different kinds of exercise affect the body. Given the assessment of the person's eating habits, the nutritionist can map out a diet that provides the nutritional balance needed to stay healthy. Depending on an individual's treatment program, there could be a need for a diet plan that changes with time.

Counseling on nutrition often benefits an individual who suffers from an eating disorder.

It may be challenging for some eating disorder patients to suddenly begin a completely new way of eating, especially if those changes initially result in weight gain. In that case, the nutritionist can recommend short-term nutritional goals and then gradually guide the patient toward long-term eating habits.

Medication

Depending on the psychological and physical effects of a patient's eating disorder, a physician may also recommend medication. Due to the link between eating disorders and depression, for example, physicians use antidepressants to treat some people with eating disorders. Antidepressant medications have proven effective in lessening or stopping binges in bulimics, and some recent studies have shown that these medications can curb binges in those with binge eating disorder. Commonly-used antidepressants include Prozac (fluoxetine), Zoloft (sertraline), and Paxil (paroxetine). Although antidepressants have been more often used to treat bulimics and binge eaters, some have also exhibited a positive effect in the treatment of anorexic patients and their ability to begin eating healthier.

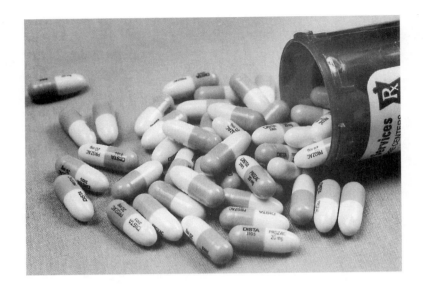

If necessary, a physician may prescribe antidepressants for an individual with an eating disorder.

Whether antidepressants or other medications are used, it is unlikely that a patient's treatment would consist solely of medications. According to one doctor, "For most patients, medication is a transitional vehicle. It can help them feel better and be less symptomatic while they are making progress in other ways. Therapy and new eating habits help patients get to a place in their lives when they may no longer require medication."[49] When patients feel better as a result of their medication, it may be easier for them to focus on other aspects of their treatment and recovery.

Hospitalization and residential care

When an eating disorder has gone untreated for an extended period, conventional therapies may no longer be sufficient. In such cases, receiving outpatient care a few times a week may not provide the supervision and treatment that the patient needs. When an eating disorder becomes life-threatening, hospitalization may be required. A hospital or residential care program provides a structured environment that makes it difficult for the person to continue his or her self-destructive behavior. During hospitalization, the person receives therapy, nutritional education, and medication. Although similar to outpatient programs, hospitalization offers more intensive treatments.

Even in the early stages of an eating disorder, hospitalization can sometimes be useful. As the authors of *Surviving an Eating Disorder* point out, "While hospitalization is essential in severe conditions, it is not always necessary to wait for such a crisis before it can be helpful. It need not be a last resort."[50]

Often the sophisticated medical resources of hospitals are not needed, and in such cases, residential care programs are an alternative to hospitalization. Such facilities provide structured recovery programs in nurturing, controlled environments. Some patients may prefer the setting of a residential care program over the hospital setting.

Recovery and relapses

According to the Center for Eating Disorders, about 60 percent of people with eating disorders can recover through treatment regimens, yet it is estimated that another 20 percent of those with eating disorders make only partial recoveries. They may respond in some ways to treatment,

Although hospitalization is sometimes necessary for treatment of severe eating disorders, it can be helpful even in less severe cases.

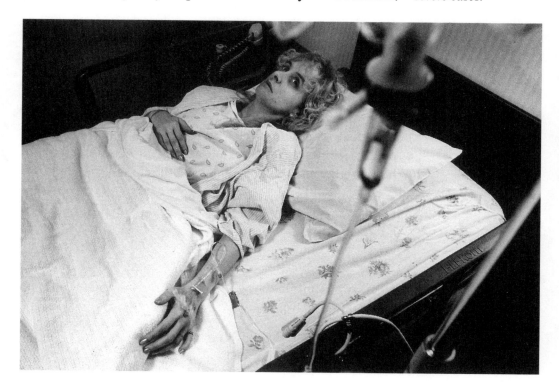

but they still fall back into old, unhealthy patterns. And even those who may seem to recover fully are still vulnerable to relapses.

Sometimes a relapse can come many years after the initial episode. One recovering anorexic suffered from the illness in her late teen years and early twenties before recovering. Then, at age thirty-four, she was diagnosed with diabetes, and her doctor recommended that she try to lose weight for health reasons. When she went on a diet, it spiraled out of control—and turned into a relapse of anorexia. As she explains,

> An eating disorder is . . . about addiction. You are addicted to starving or addicted to bingeing or addicted to bingeing and purging. Many people claim the only way to give up an addiction is to go cold turkey. Alcoholics must swear off alcohol. . . . People with eating disorders . . . can recover by staying away from any kind of dieting, vowing never to do it again.[51]

She was able to recover from the relapse, but she learned a difficult lesson in the process: "The fact is, you can have well over a decade of solid recovery, and in the span of a few seconds it can all go down the drain. It still astounds me."[52]

Approximately 20 percent of those in treatment for eating disorders do not achieve even partial recovery. They may try various programs or medical treatments, yet they are unable to break their obsession with food or weight and their struggle with low self-esteem. In light of these statistics, doctors now not only assess how to provide the best possible treatments for eating disorders but also focus on how to prevent the onset of these illnesses.

5

Preventing
Eating Disorders

EVERY PERSON'S BODY is unique. Letting go of cultural ideas about the "perfect" body is key to developing a healthy body image—and it is a crucial step in preventing eating disorders. As one doctor explains, "It's important to be realistic about yourself. . . . Many women feel that they would like their bodies if they weighed ten pounds less. Why wait to like yourself? Do your best to like and accept your body as it is now."[53]

The prevention of eating disorders also involves an increased awareness about one's relationship with food. Since dieting is so common in American culture, for some people the difference between a diet and a disorder is not perfectly clear. Often someone might be in denial about their own behavior, even when it is physically or psychologically unhealthy. For healthy dieting, it is essential to understand nutritional balance and recognize that food is not the right channel for coping with emotions.

A healthy relationship with food

A healthy attitude toward food means that a person's priority in eating is basic nourishment rather than eating for other psychological or emotional reasons. The key is understanding that a balanced diet provides the nutrients necessary for a strong, healthy body. A healthy attitude toward eating also allows for the enjoyment of particular foods—eating meals or snacks not only to satisfy hunger but also because the food tastes good.

Evaluating one's relationship with food involves reflecting on whether that relationship involves more than nutrition or enjoyment but is a source of conflict or struggle. Is food tied to one's emotions? Does eating stir up feelings of guilt or the desire to be secretive? Does food occupy one's thoughts excessively? For those who may be at risk of developing an eating disorder, and especially for people who diet, asking these questions can help to determine whether a potential problem exists.

Maintaining a healthy diet

Because so many Americans have embraced dieting almost as a way of life, it can be challenging for a person to step back and assess whether his or her relationship with food is healthy. For many people, reduced food intake has become a normal way of eating. And once a person begins dieting, even at a moderate level, he or she may not have the perspective to realize when dieting becomes obsessive. As one eating disorder therapist explains, "Unfortunately, some habits start out as once-in-a-while behaviors and turn into activities that dominate your thoughts to such an extreme that you become obsessed with them, and once obsessed you feel a compulsion or urge to do them in spite of knowing better."[54]

With so many people on diets in the United States, maintaining healthy diets—and ensuring that they do not become physically or psychologically harmful—is crucial in the prevention of eating disorders. Many therapists discourage dieting altogether since such behavior can evolve into eating disorders. But if a person must diet, the way to ensure healthy dieting is to learn about good nutrition and make an effort to practice it on a daily basis.

It is important for people on diets to step back regularly and make sure that their eating habits are healthy both physically and mentally. If they find that their eating habits are becoming a way to express feelings or seek comfort, that can be a danger sign. At that point, doctors advise that they communicate their concerns to family members or friends and get help from a professional if they are unable to break the pattern on their own.

Understanding nutrition

A carefully planned diet suited to individual needs can prevent dieting from turning into an eating disorder. It is best to avoid diets that are unsupervised or that dramatically decrease a person's food intake. A healthy diet involves choosing foods wisely for their nutritional value and eating moderate portions.

Nutritionists recommend a balanced diet from each of the five major food groups—meats, dairy, fruits, vegetables, and grains. A balanced diet ensures that the body gets all of the essential nutrients. People with special food preferences should still ensure that their diets provide complete nutrition. For example, if a person is vegetarian, he or she still needs to find other ways to consume a sufficient amount of protein. And for people with medical conditions such as diabetes or hypoglycemia, nutritional counseling can help to plan an appropriate diet that takes the condition into consideration.

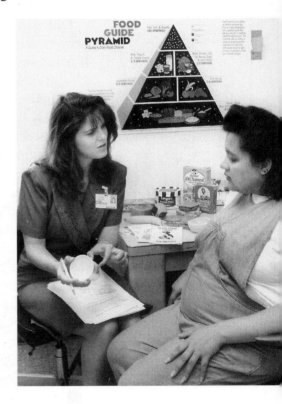

If a person wishes to lose or maintain weight through dieting, a nutritionist can give advice on how to pursue that goal in a healthy, moderate way. Professional guidance can help ensure that the diet is carefully controlled and carried out in a beneficial manner. The nutritionist can also identify a healthy weight range based on an individual's age and height, so that realistic goals are set.

Many dieters believe that drastically reducing their daily caloric intake is the best way to achieve weight loss. However, that sort of diet is usually not recommended unless endorsed by a nutritionist or other doctor. In fact, when the body's caloric intake drops significantly, the metabolism actually slows down as the body tries to conserve energy, so weight loss may not happen as rapidly as one might expect. That can lead to impatience and dissatisfaction—and, in turn, to more aggressive, unhealthy dieting.

Monitoring by a physician or nutritionist can ensure that dieting does not develop into an eating disorder.

The alternative to reduced caloric intake is, of course, increased exercise. A nutritionist or other doctor can also give feedback on whether a particular exercise program seems appropriate. Regular exercise in moderation is usually recommended. If a person wants to increase the level of exercise, then a healthy approach is to gradually increase how often and how strenuously to exercise, so that the body can naturally adjust to the program, rather than engaging in some kind of crash exercise course.

Preventing unhealthy behavior

One potential danger in dieting without professional supervision is that some diets can lead to a frequent sense of frustration. Often people set goals for reaching a particular weight or clothing size and may feel impatient about getting there. If goals are unrealistic, dissatisfaction with the results is inevitable. That dissatisfaction can lead to more anxious or obsessive dieting—and possibly the development of an eating disorder. Therefore, setting realistic goals is an important part of healthy dieting.

Because a poorly structured diet can leave a person feeling deprived and lead to bingeing, it is also important for dieters to feel satisfied by what they eat. Although diets usually involve reducing food intake, decreasing it too much could actually lead to disordered eating. Explains one doctor, "A too-skimpy diet keeps us forever hungry and dreaming of creamy concoctions. Binge eating is typically triggered by this self-starvation. Over-depriving ourselves seems to set off our body's safeguards against starvation, and it responds by wanting to eat as if there were no tomorrow."[55] Making sure that a diet provides an adequate amount of food can prevent that urge to overeat.

Unrealistic diet "deadlines" can also contribute to unhealthy dieting. Everyone's body reacts differently to weight-loss programs, and body metabolisms vary. It is hard to predict how long it will take to achieve a target weight. Such artificial deadlines can tempt a person into more aggressive dieting, rather than letting the weight loss occur at a natural pace. The result could be disordered eating. If a person has an ideal, healthy weight range in mind, it is best to think of that as a long-term goal and not set rules for how long it will take to get there.

Some eating disorder therapists recommend against frequent weighing at home, believing that the presence of a scale in the home creates an unhealthy fixation on weight reduction. When dieters weigh themselves every day or several times a day, the number on the scale can begin to dictate how they feel about themselves and their diet success. One doctor warns,

> Consider the fact that in my sixteen years of helping clients with weight control and eating disorders, I have found that those who don't weigh are the most successful. You need to learn other measures to evaluate how well you are doing. . . . Although weight changes daily owing to fluid shifts in the body, if the scale registers a one pound gain, people frequently react as though their program is not effective, they become depressed and often give up. I have seen many individuals who are on very good eating regimens become distraught if the scale doesn't show the loss in weight that they expect.[56]

The alternative to self weigh-ins is to be weighed regularly—though not too often—by a medical professional, such as a doctor or dietitian. If self weigh-ins are preferred, then doing them infrequently is the best way to judge real weight loss. This method will prevent unnecessary frustration that could eventually escalate to an eating disorder.

Separating food and weight from self-esteem

Those who study eating disorders know that many people set out to lose weight not for health reasons, but rather in an attempt to feel better about themselves. Because low self-esteem is at the heart of many eating disorders, preventing such disorders requires breaking the relationship between self-esteem and food or weight. Rather than depending on weight loss, people can find other ways to boost their self-esteem, especially by exploring personal interests or activities that make them feel positive about themselves. According to one doctor, "A well-rounded sense of self and solid self-esteem are perhaps the best antidotes to dieting and disordered eating."[57]

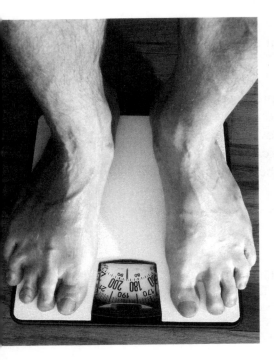

For dieters who prefer self weigh-ins, doing them infrequently is the best way to judge real weight loss.

In the case of children and teens, it is important for parents to encourage and support youngsters in ways that build self-confidence. Many doctors stress that developing positive self-esteem early in the childhood and teenage years significantly decreases the risk of developing an eating disorder. One doctor sums it up: "The most important gift adults can give children is self-esteem. . . . Self-esteem is a universal vaccine that can immunize a youngster from eating problems, body image distortion, exercise abuse, and many other problems."[58]

Emotional outlets and balance

To avoid relying on food as a way of expressing emotions, experts advise developing healthy outlets for coping with emotions or stress. Moderate exercise is one solution. Research has shown that physical exercise improves one's mood by increasing the level of serotonin in the brain. Even exercise like a brisk walk can have the desired effect.

Finding healthy emotional outlets also means making time for activities that provide satisfaction and happiness. Although work and school demands can be time-consuming, it is important to make time for activities or hobbies that are relaxing and bring personal satisfaction—whether reading a good book, drawing or painting, seeing a movie, going swimming, playing the piano, writing in a journal, or simply spending time with friends. Such activities can help to reduce stress and can also provide outlets for emotions that might otherwise be expressed through eating or dieting.

Doctors say it is helpful, too, to think about whether one's day-to-day life feels balanced in general—and if not, to think about what could change for the better. As one doctor says, "Most of us believe that a well-balanced life is important, but many of us easily forget this notion when we set about living our life. Generally speaking, a good life needs work and play, and discipline and generosity, and exercise and relaxation, and satisfaction and challenge, and togetherness and aloneness, and so on."[59]

Family influence

While verbal communication is a basic part of human interaction, it is also an important emotional outlet that can help prevent eating disorders. Communicating openly with family and friends can help express feelings that might otherwise be misdirected through disordered eating. As one recovering anorexic recalls of her treatment process "I . . . learned that I had a hard time expressing myself. . . . I'd keep everything bottled up, and bingeing and purging became the way I expressed my frustrations rather than voicing them. I became aware that I needed to say what was bothering me. Express it."[60]

The need for open communication extends to a person's home—and often that involves how parents communicate about food and body image. Because body image and ideas about food and diet are usually formed during the childhood and teenage years, conveying a healthy attitude toward food and physical appearance at home can help prevent an eating disorder later in life.

Doctors recommend that parents be careful not to overemphasize physical appearance. Praising children for losing weight may lead them to associate weight loss with self-worth. Instead, experts advise parents to teach children

Children can benefit from parental guidance on proper nutrition.

the importance of nutritionally balanced meals and the positive effects of exercise in moderation. Parents can educate and influence kids simply by practicing good nutrition in the household, thereby passing down healthy habits.

Doctors also warn against using food as a way to discipline children, such as offering treats in return for good behavior or depriving children of food in response to bad behavior. Doing so will teach children that food is always either a reward or a punishment. Rather than associating eating with positive or negative emotions, experts agree that it is better to teach youngsters that food satisfies hunger and provides nutritional value.

Parents also need to be careful when they express their own ideas about dieting to their children. When parents have a particular attitude about weight or dieting—whether it is healthy or unhealthy—that message can be conveyed subtly to children, who may take on similar views. One doctor notes this influence of adults over children: "Over the past ten years or so, the obsession with body weight and shape has become quite exaggerated in the adult population, and so you will see it affect younger and younger kids."[61]

If a child is overweight and may face potential health risks related to obesity, then a parent can try to influence the child's eating habits by encouraging sensible portions and moderate exercise rather than allowing the child to drastically reduce food intake. If that approach is not effective, then a nutritionist or dietitian should be consulted to determine an appropriate, healthy diet.

Body acceptance and a positive self-image

Rather than promoting the virtues of thinness, parents can encourage children to understand that bodies come in many different sizes and shapes. The notion that one body type is considered the "right" one is merely a myth. The myth of the perfect body is reinforced by media images of slender people. Yet if one looks around at the girls, boys, women, and men in their community, it is apparent that body types vary greatly. Body acceptance, in fact, is an essential part of preventing eating disorders.

Parental attitudes regarding physical appearance significantly influence the health of their children.

For many people, body acceptance means thinking twice before responding to the messages of the diet industry. When bombarded by so many advertisements for diet programs and products, one's body image can easily become distorted. Yet the reality is that there is no standard body type, and accepting that idea can make a person more satisfied with his or her own body shape—and less at risk of developing an eating disorder.

Building a positive self-image goes beyond body acceptance. A self-image is the total perception of oneself, including all that makes up a personal identity—character traits, values, talents, and a sense of individuality. By fixating on body image, a person can lose sight of the many nonphysical qualities that make up his or her identity. Many eating disorder therapists advise that a more well-rounded appreciation of oneself comes from recognizing how to be happy and successful independently of physical appearance. Valuing nonphysical aspects of one's identity can help a person to develop better self-esteem and a complete sense of well-being.

Raising cultural awareness

The difficulty of ignoring external appearances is clear. Images of the "ideal" body appear throughout the mass media, in magazines, movies, and television. Understanding that these images are unrealistic can enable a person to see through them and resist their claims. On an individual level, that awareness and resistance can be a powerful form of preventing eating disorders. It simply means knowing that the standard of thinness depicted in the media is not a true representation of how most people actually look.

Voicing concerns directly to the sources of those images is another form of raising awareness—one that can have a social impact. Several organizations have taken the initiative to express their views directly to the media. For example, Eating Disorders Awareness and Prevention (EDAP), a national nonprofit organization, runs a program called Giving Our Girls Inspiration and Resources for Lasting Self-Esteem! (GO GIRLS!) The semester-long program for high school girls is designed "to encourage teens to voice their opinions to advertisers, letting them know that beauty and success have little to do with the size of their jeans."[62]

With programs in various cities around the country, participants in GO GIRLS! discuss body image, eating disorders, and specifically the relationship between body image and the media. They raise peer awareness about these issues by organizing educational campaigns at local high schools. They also speak directly to the sources of the problem. They present their concerns in letters to national advertisers and presentations to retail corporation executives. The project gives participants a chance to rally against the mass media's negative impact on body image.

GO GIRLS! is just one example of an organized program for building teens' awareness of the media's impact on body image. Many other organizations have similar campaigns, either on a local or a national level. However, anyone can take the initiative to express his or her views and raise awareness. Communicating one's opinions could mean simply writing a letter to an advertiser or a corpora-

Reprinted by permission of Kirk Anderson.

tion whose messages have a negative impact on body image. By voicing those concerns, individuals can help to influence the images that eventually reach millions of people and, in turn, help to promote positive body images.

The increasing need for prevention

As eating disorders have become a growing health problem in the United States, prevention has become a mounting concern. Of particular concern is the spread of eating disorders to younger people. Doctors report that the average age of those with eating disorders is dropping, with the problem even affecting children in elementary school.

While expanding resources can benefit those suffering from eating disorders, doctors feel that the need for prevention has become more urgent. As more people become aware of why eating disorders develop, who is at risk, and ways to prevent these illnesses, they can help each other—and themselves—to maintain healthy habits and cultivate positive self-images.

WATERLOO HIGH SCHOOL LIBRARY
1464 INDUSTRY RD.
ATWATER, OH 44201

Notes

Chapter 1: An Obsession with Food

1. Michele Siegel, Judith Brisman, and Margot Weinshel, *Surviving an Eating Disorder: Strategies for Family and Friends*. New York: HarperPerennial, 1997, pp. 6–7.

2. Quoted in Ira M. Sacker and Marc A. Zimmer, *Dying to Be Thin: Understanding and Defeating Anorexia Nervosa and Bulimia—A Practical, Lifesaving Guide*. New York: Warner Books, 1987, p. 50.

3. Mary Pipher, *Reviving Ophelia: Saving the Selves of Adolescent Girls*. New York: Ballantine Books, 1994, pp. 174–75.

4. Quoted in Carolyn Costin, *Your Dieting Daughter: Is She Dying for Attention?* New York: Brunner/Mazel, 1997, p. 17.

5. Quoted in Siegel, Brisman, and Weinshel, *Surviving an Eating Disorder*, pp. 19–20.

6. Quoted in Sacker and Zimmer, *Dying to Be Thin*, p. 58.

7. Brett Valette, *A Parent's Guide to Eating Disorders: Prevention and Treatment of Anorexia Nervosa and Bulimia*. New York: Walker, 1988, p. 64.

8. Quoted in Kim Hubbard, Anne-Marie O'Neill, and Christina Cheakalos, "Out of Control," *People*, April 12, 1999, p. 56.

9. Quoted in Costin, *Your Dieting Daughter*, p. 21.

10. Quoted in Dixie Farley, "Eating Disorders: When Thinness Becomes an Obsession," *FDA Consumer*, U.S. Food and Drug Administration, HHS Publication No. (FDA) 86-2211, May 1986. www.nau.edu/fronske/eatdis.html.

11. James E. Mitchell, ed., *Anorexia Nervosa and Bulimia: Diagnosis and Treatment*. Minneapolis: University of Minnesota Press, 1985, p. 37.

12. Quoted in Pipher, *Reviving Ophelia*, p. 170.

13. Quoted in Sacker and Zimmer, *Dying to Be Thin*, p. 27.

14. Quoted in Suzanne Abraham and Derek Llewellyn-Jones, *Eating Disorders: The Facts*. 4th ed. Oxford, England: Oxford University Press, 1997, p. 202.

15. Siegel, Brisman, and Weinshel, *Surviving an Eating Disorder*, p. 33.

16. Quoted in Laurie Tarkan, "Diary of an Eating Disorder," *Shape*, November 1998, p. 138.

Chapter 2: The Causes and Risk Factors of Eating Disorders

17. Quoted in Judith Newman, "Girls Who Won't Eat: The Alarming New Epidemic of Eating Disorders," *Redbook*, October 1997, p. 152.

18. Quoted in Deborah Haber, "A Body to Die For," *Self*, February 1999, p. 129.

19. Quoted in Haber, "A Body to Die For," p. 130.

20. Quoted in Sara Shandler, *Ophelia Speaks: Adolescent Girls Write About Their Search for Self*. New York: Harper-Perennial, 1999, p. 24.

21. Quoted in Abraham and Llewellyn-Jones, *Eating Disorders*, p. 107.

22. Mary Pipher, *Hunger Pains: The Modern Woman's Tragic Quest for Thinness*. New York: Ballantine Books, 1997, p. 72.

23. Quoted in Peggy Claude-Pierre, *The Secret Language of Eating Disorders: How You Can Understand and Work to Cure Anorexia and Bulimia*. New York: Vintage Books, 1997, p. 242.

24. Quoted in Newman, "Girls Who Won't Eat," p. 122.

25. Quoted in Valette, *A Parent's Guide to Eating Disorders*, pp. 48–49.

26. Claude-Pierre, *The Secret Language of Eating Disorders*, p. 74.

27. Marcia Millman, *Such a Pretty Face: Being Fat in America*. New York: Berkley Books, 1980, p. 216.

28. Jeanne Brooks-Gunn and Anne C. Petersen, eds., *Girls at Puberty: Biological and Psychosocial Perspective*. New York: Plenum, 1983, p. 145.

29. Quoted in Lindsey Hall and Leigh Cohn, eds., *Recoveries: True Stories by People Who Conquered Addictions and Compulsions*. Carlsbad, CA: Gürze Books, 1987, p. 43.

30. Lauren Slater, "I Thought It Couldn't Happen Again," *Health*, October 1998, p. 116.

31. Quoted in Hubbard, O'Neill, and Cheakalos, "Out of Control," p. 54.

32. Anorexia Nervosa and Related Eating Disorders, Inc. "Athletes with Eating Disorders: Overview," 1998. www.anred.com/ath-intro.html.

33. Quoted in Anorexia Nervosa and Related Eating Disorders, Inc., "Athletes with Eating Disorders."

34. Quoted in Pipher, *Reviving Ophelia*, p. 166.

Chapter 3: The Effects of Eating Disorders

35. Sacker and Zimmer, *Dying to Be Thin*, p. 22.

36. Quoted in Hubbard, O'Neill, and Cheakalos, "Out of Control," p. 69.

37. B. Timothy Walsh and Michael J. Devlin, "Eating Disorders: Progress and Problems," *Science*, May 29, 1998, p. 1388.

38. Quoted in Sacker and Zimmer, *Dying to Be Thin*, p. 35.

39. Quoted in Christine Gorman, "Disappearing Act," *Time*, November 2, 1998, p. 110.

40. Pipher, *Hunger Pains*, p. 65.

41. Quoted in Nancy J. Kolodny, *When Food's a Foe: How You Can Confront and Conquer Your Eating Disorder*. 2nd rev. ed. Boston: Little, Brown, 1998, p. 38.

42. Quoted in Haber, "A Body to Die For," p. 130.

Chapter 4: Treating Eating Disorders

43. American Anorexia Bulimia Association, Inc., "Information for Family and Friends," September 1999. Available from www.aabainc.org/familyfriends/index.html.

44. Quoted in Farley, "Eating Disorders."

45. Quoted in Emily Haigh, "Noted Psychotherapist to Lecture on Eating Disorders," *Chronicle,* February 25, 1994. www.chronicle.duke.edu/chronicle/94/02/25/1eating.html.

46. *Reflections,* "Breaking away from Tradition—Experiential Therapies for Eating Disorders and Weight Preoccupation," Spring 1998. www.ams.queensu.ca/anab/news0498. htm#break.

47. Valette, *A Parent's Guide to Eating Disorders*, p. 103.

48. Millman, *Such a Pretty Face*, p. 32.

49. Diane Mickley, "Eating Disorders and Antidepressants: Answers to the Most Commonly Asked Questions," American Anorexia Bulimia Association, Inc., October 1999, p. 3.

50. Siegel, Brisman, and Weinshel, *Surviving an Eating Disorder*, p. 148.

51. Slater, "I Thought It Couldn't Happen Again," p. 95.

52. Slater, "I Thought It Couldn't Happen Again," p. 95.

Chapter 5: Preventing Eating Disorders

53. Pipher, *Hunger Pains*, p. 97.

54. Kolodny, *When Food's a Foe*, p. 29.

55. Valette, *A Parent's Guide to Eating Disorders*, p. 25.

56. Costin, *Your Dieting Daughter*, pp. 156–57.

57. Michael Levine, "Ten Things Parents Can Do to Help Prevent Eating Disorders." Seattle: Eating Disorders Awareness and Prevention, Inc., 1999. (Originally presented at the Thirteenth National NEDO Conference, Columbus, OH, October 3, 1994.)

58. Paula Levine, "Prevention Guidelines and Strategies for Everyone: Fifty Ways to Lose the '3-D's': Dieting, Drive for Thinness, and Body Dissatisfaction." Seattle: Eating Disorders Awareness and Prevention, Inc., 1999.

59. Kathy Bowen-Woodward, *Coping with a Negative Body-Image*. New York: Rosen, 1989, p. 105.

60. Quoted in Tarkan, "Diary of an Eating Disorder," p. 141.

61. Quoted in Newman, "Girls Who Won't Eat," p. 123.

62. Eating Disorders Awareness and Prevention, Inc., "GO GIRLS!" August 1999. www.edap.org.

Organizations
to Contact

American Anorexia Bulimia Association, Inc. (AABA)
165 W. 46th St. #1108
New York, NY 10036
(212) 575-6200
website: www.aabainc.org

This national nonprofit organization is committed to the prevention and treatment of eating disorders through education, advocacy, and research. AABA services include referral networks, public information, school outreach, media support, professional training, support groups, and prevention programs.

**Anorexia Nervosa and Related Eating Disorders, Inc.
(ANRED)**
website: www.anred.com

ANRED is a nonprofit organization that operates an educational website with information about eating disorders. The website is updated monthly and covers a wide range of topics related to the causes, effects, treatment, and prevention of eating disorders. ANRED is affiliated with Eating Disorders Awareness and Prevention, Inc.

Eating Disorders Awareness and Prevention, Inc. (EDAP)
603 Stewart St., Suite 803
Seattle, WA 98101
(206) 382-3587
website: www.edap.org

This national nonprofit organization is "dedicated to increasing awareness and prevention of eating disorders through education and community activism." It offers educational materials to the public and has a toll-free information and resource line (800-931-2237) for those struggling with eating disorders, friends and family of people with eating disorders, educators, and health professionals. EDAP sponsors a National Eating Disorders Awareness Week every year in February. It has developed a national media advocacy campaign to raise awareness about the media's impact on body image as well as the GO GIRLS! program for high school girls.

Gürze Books
PO Box 2238
Carlsbad, CA 92018
(800) 756-7533
website: www.gurze.com

Gürze Books publishes an *Eating Disorders Resource Catalogue*, which includes an extensive offering of books on eating disorders as well as listings of treatment facilities. The catalog, available by calling the toll-free number above, is also distributed by therapists, support groups, college health and counseling centers, and eating disorder conferences and workshops. Gürze Books is involved with the recovery, research, education, advocacy, and prevention of eating disorders.

Massachusetts Eating Disorders Association, Inc. (MEDA)
92 Pearl St.
Newton, MA 02158
(617) 558-1881
website: www.medainc.org

This organization's goal is "to help nurture the self-esteem of children so they will learn to value themselves based on their inner worth as individuals, rather than external appearance." The largest provider of outpatient support services in the Northeast, MEDA offers a referral network, local support groups, and educational materials. It also raises community and national awareness through seminars, conferences, and presentations to schools and businesses.

National Association of Anorexia Nervosa and Associated Disorders (ANAD)

PO Box 7
Highland Park, IL 60035
(847) 831-3438
website: www.anad.org

This national nonprofit organization helps those with eating disorders and their families. They offer counseling through a national hot line (phone number listed above), which can provide a listing of support groups and referrals to therapists and hospitals in an individual's local area. ANAD also makes information packets available to the public and organizes national conferences and local programs to promote education on eating disorders. The organization develops research projects and organizes advocacy campaigns to protect potential victims of eating disorders.

Overeaters Anonymous (OA)

PO Box 44020
Rio Rancho, NM 87174-4020
(505) 891-2664
website: www.overeatersanonymous.org

The OA fellowship is open to anyone recovering from compulsive overeating (binge eating). Members follow a twelve-step program to recover from compulsive overeating while sharing support with each other. There are no dues or fees for members to attend meetings in their local area. The main headquarters (listed above) can provide information on where local meetings take place. These listings may also appear in the local phone book.

Suggestions for Further Reading

Kathy Bowen-Woodward, *Coping with a Negative Body-Image*. New York: Rosen, 1989. Written primarily for and about girls, this book discusses how a negative body image can develop and provides suggestions for how to improve it. Each chapter contains exercises that help readers to think about their own body image.

Nancy J. Kolodny, *When Food's a Foe: How You Can Confront and Conquer Your Eating Disorder.* 2nd rev. ed. Boston: Little, Brown, 1998. A self-help guide offering information on how eating disorders develop, their impact on a person's life, how they can be treated, and ways to prevent them.

Steven Levenkron, *The Best Little Girl in the World*. New York: Warner Books, 1978. A best-selling novel for young readers, this book tells the story of a girl who battles anorexia nervosa, an obsession with losing weight that becomes self-destructive.

Ira M. Sacker and Marc A. Zimmer, *Dying to Be Thin: Understanding and Defeating Anorexia Nervosa and Bulimia—A Practical, Lifesaving Guide*. New York: Warner Books, 1987. A comprehensive resource about the causes, symptoms, and treatment options for eating disorders. The authors present first-person accounts of eating disorder patients as well as their doctors, families, and friends.

Laura Weeldreyer, *Body Blues: Weight and Depression*. New York: Rosen, 1998. This educational book explores how a negative body image can lead to depression. It also offers possible ways to lift the "body blues," whether by helping oneself or seeking help from others.

Works Consulted

Books

Suzanne Abraham and Derek Llewellyn-Jones, *Eating Disorders: The Facts*. 4th ed. Oxford, England: Oxford University Press, 1997. An educational book on anorexia, bulimia, and obesity. Topics include why eating disorders develop, the characteristics and behaviors of each type of disorder, diagnosis, and treatment.

Jeanne Brooks-Gunn and Anne C. Petersen, eds., *Girls at Puberty: Biological and Psychosocial Perspective*. New York: Plenum, 1983. A collection of research-based essays from a medical perspective. Covers biological, psychological, and sociocultural aspects of girls during puberty.

Peggy Claude-Pierre, *The Secret Language of Eating Disorders: How You Can Understand and Work to Cure Anorexia and Bulimia*. New York: Vintage Books, 1997. The author, the founder of an eating disorder treatment program, presents her own insights into the causes of anorexia and bulimia, explains the basis of her treatment program, and offers some inspiring stories of those in recovery.

Carolyn Costin, *Your Dieting Daughter: Is She Dying for Attention?* New York: Brunner/Mazel, 1997. Written specifically for parents of daughters with eating disorders, this informative book clarifies the distinction between a diet and a disorder, examines popular diets, offers helpful nutritional facts, and includes personal anecdotes from girls who diet and their parents.

Lindsey Hall and Leigh Cohn, eds., *Recoveries: True Stories by People Who Conquered Addictions and Compulsions*.

Carlsbad, CA: Gürze Books, 1987. A collection of personal stories about survival and recovery from various addictions and compulsions. The personal essays include one woman's story of recovery from anorexia and another woman's account of recovery from bulimia.

Marcia Millman, *Such a Pretty Face: Being Fat in America.* New York: Berkley Books, 1980. A look at how obesity is perceived by American society. Topics include how being fat affects one's self-perception, how it shapes one's social identity, and the varied effects of obesity on females and males.

James E. Mitchell, ed., *Anorexia Nervosa and Bulimia: Diagnosis and Treatment.* Minneapolis: University of Minnesota Press, 1985. An overview of anorexia and bulimia diagnosis and treatment, presented from a research-based, medical perspective.

Mary Pipher, *Hunger Pains: The Modern Woman's Tragic Quest for Thinness.* New York: Ballantine Books, 1997. Focuses on the American obsession with physical appearance and how that significantly affects body acceptance for girls and women. Includes discussions of eating disorders, interesting case examples, and practical advice on how to find peace with one's body.

———, *Reviving Ophelia: Saving the Selves of Adolescent Girls.* New York: Ballantine Books, 1994. A powerful look at the personal and cultural issues that challenge adolescent girls today—issues that ultimately damage their sense of self—and what adults can do to help, both on a personal level and by changing American culture.

Sara Shandler, *Ophelia Speaks: Adolescent Girls Write About Their Search for Self.* New York: HarperPerennial, 1999. A unique collection of firsthand writings from adolescent girls around America, speaking from a variety of backgrounds. Each chapter addresses a different issue facing girls today as well as the author's personal reflections on the topic.

Michele Siegel, Judith Brisman, and Margot Weinshel, *Surviving an Eating Disorder: Strategies for Family and Friends*. New York: HarperPerennial, 1997. A useful book designed to help the family and friends of those struggling with eating disorders. Offers advice on detecting eating disorders, includes case examples, and explains how to guide a family member or friend toward treatment and through the recovery process.

Brett Valette, *A Parent's Guide to Eating Disorders: Prevention and Treatment of Anorexia Nervosa and Bulimia*. New York: Walker, 1988. A helpful resource for parents whose children suffer from eating disorders. Clearly explains why eating disorders develop, how to detect warning signs, and various treatment options.

Periodicals

Christine Gorman, "Disappearing Act," *Time*, November 2, 1998.

Deborah Haber, "A Body to Die For," *Self*, February 1999.

Kim Hubbard, Anne-Marie O'Neill, and Christina Cheakalos, "Out of Control," *People*, April 12, 1999.

Judith Newman, "Girls Who Won't Eat: The Alarming New Epidemic of Eating Disorders," *Redbook*, October 1997.

Tamara Pryor and Michael W. Wiederman, "Personality Features and Expressed Concerns of Adolescents with Eating Disorders," *Adolescence*, Summer 1998.

Barbara J. Rolls, Dianne Engell, and Leann L. Birch, "Serving Portion Size Influences Five-Year-Old but Not Three-Year-Old Children's Food Intakes," *Journal of the American Dietetic Association*, February 2000.

Lauren Slater, "I Thought It Couldn't Happen Again," *Health*, October 1998.

Laurie Tarkan, "Diary of an Eating Disorder," *Shape*, November 1998.

B. Timothy Walsh and Michael J. Devlin, "Eating Disorders: Progress and Problems," *Science*, May 29, 1998.

Internet Sources

American Anorexia Bulimia Association, Inc., "Information for Family and Friends," September 1999. www.aabainc.org/familyfriends/index.html.

Anorexia Nervosa and Related Eating Disorders, Inc., "Athletes with Eating Disorders: Overview," 1998. www.anred.com/ath-intro.html.

Center for Eating Disorders, "Frequently Asked Questions," September 1999. www.eatingdisorder.org.

Eating Disorders Awareness and Prevention, Inc., "GO GIRLS!" August 1999. www.edap.org.

Dixie Farley, "Eating Disorders: When Thinness Becomes an Obsession," *FDA Consumer*, U.S. Food and Drug Administration, HHS Publication No. (FDA) 86-2211, May 1986. www.nau.edu/fronske/eatdis.html.

Emily Haigh, "Noted Psychotherapist to Lecture on Eating Disorders," *Chronicle*, February 25, 1994. www. chronicle.duke.edu/chronicle/94/02/25/1eating.html.

Laureate Eating Disorders Program, "Anorexia Nervosa: Warning Signs," August 2000. http://216.234.238.229/ behavioralhealth/ed/abouted/anorexia.asp.

———, "Binge Eating Disorder: Warning Signs," August 2000. http://216.234.238.229/behavioralhealth/ed/abouted/ binge.asp.

———, "Bulimia Nervosa: Warning Signs," August 2000. http://216.234.238.229/behavioralhealth/ed/abouted/ bulimianerv.asp.

Reflections, "Breaking away from Tradition—Experiential Therapies for Eating Disorders and Weight Preoccupation," Spring 1998. www.ams.queensu.ca/anab/news0498.htm#break.

Educational Materials

Michael Levine, "Ten Things Parents Can Do to Help Prevent Eating Disorders." Seattle: Eating Disorders Awareness and Prevention, Inc., 1999. (Originally presented at the Thirteenth National NEDO Conference, Columbus, OH, October 3, 1994.)

Paula Levine, "Prevention Guidelines and Strategies for Everyone: Fifty Ways to Lose the '3-D's': Dieting, Drive for Thinness, and Body Dissatisfaction." Seattle: Eating Disorders Awareness and Prevention, Inc., 1999.

Diane Mickley, "Eating Disorders and Antidepressants: Answers to the Most Commonly Asked Questions," American Anorexia Bulimia Association, Inc., October 1999.

Index

Picture Credits

Cover photo: Richard T. Nowitz/ASAP/Photo Researchers
Corbis/Richard T. Nowitz, 29, 56, 60
Corbis/Scott Roper, 53
Impact Visuals, 7, 12, 15, 59, 64, 65, 69
Photo Disc, 18, 23, 26, 31, 33, 35, 39, 72, 73, 75
Photo Researchers, 20, 63

About the Author

Jennifer L. Strada is a writer and editor who has worked in book publishing for several years. She currently lives in San Francisco, where she is a production editor at an educational publishing company.

This book may be kept

FOURTEEN DAYS

A fine will be charged for each day the book is kept overtime.

3-4-03			
3-4-04			
1-28-05			
2/18/05			
2-9-05			
GAYLORD 142			PRINTED IN U.S.A.